CHILD AND ADOLESCENT TREATMENT
for
SOCIAL WORK PRACTICE

A Relational Perspective for Beginning Clinicians

Theresa Aiello, Ph.D.

THE FREE PRESS

The Free Press
A Division of Simon & Schuster
1230 Avenue of the Americas
New York, NY 10020

Designed by MM Design 2000 Inc.

Manufactured in the United States of America

10 9 8 7 6 5 4 3 2 1

Library of Congress Cataloging-In-Publication Data

Aiello, Theresa.
        Child and adolescent treatment for social work practice : a
Relational perspective for beginning clinicians / Theresa Aiello.
        p. cm
        Includes bibliographical references and index.
        1. Social work with children.   2. Social work with youth.
3. Psychiatric social work.   I. Title.
HV713.A39   1999   99-17092   CIP
362.7—dc21

ISBN: 0-7432-3788-9

For information regarding special discounts for bulk purchases, please contact Simon &
Schuster Special Sales at 1-800-456-6798 or business@simonandschuster.com

CONTENTS

Acknowledgments   vii

Introduction   x

PART I • THE BEGINNING PHASE OF TREATMENT

1. Relational Theory in the Treatment of Children   3

2. Relational Theory in the Treatment of Adolescents   12

3. Diagnostic Assessment of Children   29

4. Diagnostic Assessment of Adolescents   33

5. The Initial Session   40

6. Play Therapy   57

7. Psychopathology of Childhood and Adolescence   72

8. Posttraumatic Stress Disorder   83

9. Learning Disabilities   97

PART II • THE MIDDLE PHASE OF TREATMENT

10. Transference   103

11. Countertransference   113

**PART III • MAJOR THEMES IN CLINICAL SOCIAL WORK
WITH CHILDREN AND ADOLESCENTS**

12. Physical Illness, Death, and Dying   125

13. Sexuality and Sexual Orientation   132

14. Foster Care   139

15. Adoption   144

16. Multicultural Issues   149

PART IV • THERAPEUTIC MODALITIES
AND SPECIAL PROGRAMS

17. Family Treatment   159

18. Residential Treatment and Day Treatment   168

19. Group Treatment with Children   177

20. Group Treatment with Adolescents   196

PART V • TERMINATION

21. The Termination Process   201

Bibliography   205

Index   213

ACKNOWLEDGMENTS

Writing a book of this sort is a kind of clinical autobiography stretching across approximately twenty-five years of practice. It goes without saying that while I wrote this, the spirits of many children crowded around, providing me, as always, with their cheerful, irreverent, and impudent comments, entertaining me with "wisecracks," as they would say; they reminded me relentlessly of how I might have done better and of when I did well enough, whether in treatment or in teaching and supervising their therapists. They get the first acknowledgment.

I would like to express my appreciation to my colleagues at New York University Ehrenkranz School of Social Work. Deans Thomas Meenaghan, Eleanore Korman, and Lucretia Phillips have provided me with a supportive and congenial environment to work in.

My colleague Dr. Eda Goldstein, director of the NYU Ph.D. program, provided me with mentorship and her experience and wisdom about writing. Dr. George Frank, professor emeritus and founding director of the NYU Ph.D. program, practical humanist, was, as always, an invaluable source of inspiration and support. First as student and then as colleague, I had much to learn from both of them.

I would like to thank Dr. Judith Marks Mishne for her generous erudition in matters of child treatment. Drs. Gladys Gonzalez Ramos, Mary Ellen Noonan, Carol Tosone, and Rena Greenblatt and Prof. Milly Sanchez Krappaff have listened to sections of this book and provided important insights. Over the years I have benefited from many discussions on theory and practice with my friend and colleague Dr. Jeff Seinfeld. I wish to express my gratitude to several teachers and supervisors at the Jewish Board of Family and Children Services. I owe a great debt of gratitude to Eugene Glynn, M.D. His example as teacher, mentor, and role model was an enormous source of inspiration to me. He has set a standard that I continually strive to emulate. I owe a great deal to Patrica Nitzberg, CSW, and Myrna Epstein, MSW, for their teaching, supervision, and generosity in sharing their clinical knowledge of children.

I am particularly indebted to Dr. William Reulbach, whose friendship and dedication to his work have become an invaluable source of inspiration to me. His clinical work has helped to enliven these pages.

Ms. Susan Anthony, Dr. Jean Bailey, Dr. Linda Apsel, Ms. Jo Bellamo, Ms. Patrica Hill, Dr. Diane Tirado-Lampert, Greg Pagano, CSW, Ms. Ana dela Rosa, CSW, Ms. Doris Goldman, CSW, Ms. Diana Cavallo, Keith Schenenga, CSW, Barbara Schuster, MSW, Curtis Brown, CSW, and Paul Jaffe, CSW, are a circle of friends who are also colleagues, entwined by our work; their spirits and examples of their clinical practice also enliven these pages. I owe thanks to Phillip Rappaport, my editor, whose belief in this first book enabled it to come to fruition. I would also like to thank the editorial staff of the Free Press for their patient and thoughtful editing skills.

I would like to express my gratitude to Andrew Schmidt and Angela DeLuca, who are at the beginning of their social work careers, for their editorial skill and assistance, and to Richard Lenert, who has been an invaluable source of help throughout my years at NYU.

My gratitude to my family, Salvatore and Lucy Aiello and Josephine Suozzo, and especially to my sister and best friend, Angela Aiello.

Dr. Thomas Belmonte could not live to see the end of this work. His spirit nonetheless stands by me while I write—*fra noi.*

My appreciation to Dr. Larry Lockridge for his support, his music, and his laughter.

To the memory of my brother, Sal Aiello, my first friend, and to all the children and their social workers in this book.

VOICES

Ideal and dearly beloved voices
of those who are dead, or those
who are lost to us like the dead.
Sometimes they speak to us in our dreams;
Sometimes in thought the mind hears them.
And for a moment with their echo other echoes
return from the first poetry of our lives—
like music that extinguishes the far-off night.

C. P. Cavafy
Translated by Rae Dalven

INTRODUCTION

This book is written for clinicians at the very beginning of their work in social service settings.

Childhood is a fairly recent invention (Aries, 1962). Prior to the first child labor laws in England and America, children were subjected to great abuses and held to the same standards and laws by which adults were judged. Unfortunately, today most of the old injustices still exist and challenge more than ever those of us who work with children. Physical and sexual abuse; substance abuse; deprivation, both emotional and material, and the conditions that produce it; and, most recently, AIDS, one of the single greatest world epidemics since the plague—all deeply affect the children and families that we routinely see in social work agencies. All have the components or sequelae of trauma. Today many of those clinicians who work in mental health with these populations experience secondary trauma and burnout syndrome.

There are many great psychoanalytic and systemic models to explain and conceptualize human behavior, but the question my students ask over and over is, How can we translate these theories into plain, practical speech that is useful to our clients?

In my first career I was a musician. The best example of how to play music was to begin by demonstration. The music students would get the sound of a phrase in their ear and imitate the teacher or master performer. Later on, they could weave their own individuality into the music. This blending of the voice of the teacher with one's own idiosyncratic talents and tastes was the result of a slow integration, gained over time with patience and practice. I have written this text with this principle very much in mind. By using real (and often dramatic) cases from my own and my students' experiences in social service settings, I have attempted to give the "sound" of interventions and interpretations along with their theoretical explanations.

I do think that much of what I've gathered here can be easily critiqued, but therapeutic practice is not a science. It is, rather, more of an art that is deeply human in its origins and hence deeply relational. I would hope that over time readers of this text will find and develop their own voices and feel confident enough to use them. At the very beginning, however, it helps to have other voices to guide one in the process of learning how to be a therapist. The beauty of the psychoanalytic tradition is in that continuation of voice that is passed from teacher to student to client. Though mutated over time and tempered by recent findings, research, and conceptualizations, it continues, hopefully, to reflect as much of the truth as possible.

It may well be that social workers invented psychotherapy in America. They were the first to work with the poor, the disaffiliated, and the oppressed, with children and their families. In addition to addressing social conditions, they sought to address the psychological conditions that accompany all of us in all of our travails (Aiello, 1998).

An important relational principle is that of mutual self- and object-regulation while attempting to maintain a balanced, essentially positive sense of self-esteem (self-regulation) simultaneously. This process is mutual in nature.

Psychoanalysis has greatly influenced and enriched clinical social work. In turn, clinical social work has begun to influence psychoanalysis, both in theory and in practice. This is already evidenced by the recent interest of psychoanalysts in multiculturalism, intersubjectivity, gender and sexual-orientation differences, social class, linguistics, and, in particular, the reexamination of the importance of the narrative with an emphasis on the right to personal autonomy. All of these are old social work principles that take on new and ever-evolving life in the welding together of a social work praxis with theory.

I believe that the recently emerging constructs of relational theory, as written by Stephen Mitchell and others, have best integrated the most salient psychoanalytic and developmental concepts. These reflect concepts gathered from across the psychoanalytic canon—in particular, the independent tradition, self psychology, and, most recently, infant research. I agree with Mitchell and others that psychoanalysis is best viewed as a social theory.

Social work practice in general is, however, not represented by one single theory but, rather, by a great many social and psychodynamic concepts. How appropriate, then, to weld this rendering of psychoanalysis together with social work practice with children.

Child treatment has had its own golden age of theory and practice—from Anna Freud and Melanie Klein, through the British independent tradition and ego psychology, to the best family theorists. A host of important writers and researchers emerged, and yet child treatment still somehow seems to be a stepchild of psychoanalysis. Early narrative historical accounts of child therapy in America often cite child treatment as a somehow less important, less demanding specialty. In a number of accounts from the pioneers in psychoanalysis, we find that the treatment of children was often left to the wives of analysts (Menaker, 1989; Mahler, 1988).

It is probably no accident that the child became an important early focus in social work (a profession much dominated by women). Children are the least vocal members of society, relying upon adults to speak to their needs and to care for them. Social workers historically were among the first to advocate and represent children and families within social welfare programs, in the child guidance movement, and in the settlement houses.

This is still true today. I very much believe in the integrity of both social work and psychoanalysis and have attempted here to produce a text that is both simple and practical for beginners. This textbook attempts to apply relational theory to clinical social work practice with children. Utilizing case material, I hope to clarify and illustrate concepts as they appear in direct practice. In it I have reflected, wherever possible, what I believe are important current theoretical and developmental principles, but I have coupled these with direct practice scenarios and interventions from clinic populations.

When I was a very young and inexperienced child therapist at the beginning of my training, I made an important personal discovery. One day the child care staff of our residential treatment facility commented to the therapists on the different styles of the psychotherapy staff. They noted that each therapist's personal style left a kind of individual, distinctive stamp on the children he or she had treated. For example, a colleague of mine, a gifted young social worker, had difficulty expressing anger and had recently entered into treatment herself. Although her eyes would often fill with tears when she was angry in her personal life, as a therapist she remained composed and conscientious. She had a great ability to work with extremely aggressive, abusive children, and she could tolerate their oftentimes repugnant rages, which included vitriolic verbal attacks on her. The child care staff noted that her "children" had a distinct ability to label their anger and to express this articulately. It was pointed out to me that my "children" were particularly good at analyzing cause and effect to explain their feelings and behaviors. Both my colleague and I felt greatly rewarded by these developments in the children we treated. The best any therapist can do is to help clients articulate their feelings rather than act on them destructively. From the perspective of our work, this meant the beginnings of self-understanding for our child patients and, hence, of an ability to become self-regulating at a higher level. The move away from action and impulse to self-reflection enabled a new linguistic ability to develop: the ability to label feelings, to put feelings into words. Winnicott described the holding environment as the therapist's ability to help the patient tolerate and describe the deepest level of anxiety and to verbally amplify upon unconscious and conscious interpretations.

My colleague and I didn't know at the time, except in perhaps a lucky, unconscious sense, that this was somehow the right way to work. I was bringing my own love of understanding and analyzing behavior to my child patients without knowing it. I think my colleague realized then that we had stumbled upon an important discovery, namely, that clinicians do indeed have an impact on clients, that a piece of ourselves, however minimal, goes on to influence the people we see in practice.

We therapists will, however, never completely know what piece of ourselves will necessarily be selected to be identified with. With full knowledge of the weight of this responsibility, I hope that this volume will assist the reader in developing the right balance of consciousness, knowledge, and use of the gifts of individuality in becoming a child therapist and, in turn, in helping others.

This volume contains many descriptive vignettes of the kinds of treatment problems that child therapists routinely encounter in child guidance facilities. I have deliberately focused more on child treatment techniques than on family therapy. In my attempt to own my own theoretical biases, I well acknowledge that I believe children (and adolescents) today present more complex difficulties than ever before. The severity of the cases I have selected for this volume warranted individual work, with family therapy as a conjoint modality. When children and their families have difficulties as severe as those presented in these cases, family sessions often give short shrift to children.

Cicero once said that a society that does not value its youth has no future. I believe that therapists who work with children must address their needs as attentively as those of their parents.

THE ORGANIZATION OF THE TEXT

As this book emphasizes practice techniques with children and adolescents, all chapters include case vignettes. These vignettes illustrate an integration of theoretical concepts with the practice of technique. They by no means present cure-alls; rather, they attempt to illuminate the actual treatment process and to elucidate theory as it is illustrated in practice.

Part I: The Beginning Phase of Treatment

Chapters 1 and 2 outline the concepts, origins, and theoretical underpinnings of relational theory—ego psychology, self psychology, and object relations theory from psychoanalysis; systems theory; and developmental theory.

Chapters 3 and 4 present the format and practice principles utilized in the diagnostic assessment of children and adolescents. Chapter 5 presents examples of the initial session in light of the assessment process. Chapter 6 illustrates play therapy principles and techniques.

Chapter 7 discusses psychopathology as it is typically encountered in child and adolescent clients. Since so much of psychopathology emanates from trauma, an entire chapter, Chapter 8, is devoted to a discussion of posttraumatic stress syndrome and the concepts of and research on trauma theory. Chapter 9 discusses assessment and treatment issues involved in work with children and adolescents diagnosed with learning disabilities.

Part II: The Middle Phase of Treatment

Part II describes the evolving relationship between therapist and child. In Chapters 10 and 11, transference and countertransference phenomena are discussed. Theoretical concepts are applied in understanding the typical practice problems and countertransference/transference reactions that emanate from psychotherapy.

Part III: General Therapeutic Issues in the Treatment
of Children and Adolescents

Chapter 12 examines the problems of physical illness, death, and dying in the treatment of children and adolescents.

Chapter 13 focuses on sexuality and sexual orientation. The discussion of the coming-out process for gay adolescents utilizes concepts from social constructivist theorists and relational writing on gender.

Clinical approaches to child welfare issues, in particular, work with children in foster care, are the focus for Chapter 14. Chapter 15 reviews typical themes of treatment that arise in work with adopted children.

Chapter 16 discusses issues of culture, race, and ethnicity as they emerge in psychotherapy, with particular attention to the subjective experience of racial or cultural difference between child and therapist.

Part IV: Therapeutic Modalities and Special Programs

Chapter 17 focuses on family treatment for the single-parent family (the most commonly encountered family type in social service settings and the one with the most severe stressors).

Chapter 18 examines the special uses of the milieu therapy in residential and day treatment programs for children who cannot be managed in regular school classes.

Chapters 19 and 20 examine group treatment for children and adolescents, respectively. This modality is regularly utilized in school and community programs.

Part V: Termination

The final chapter, Chapter 21, focuses on the end of treatment. It deals with the termination process, gift giving as an offer of a transitional object, and determining when termination is appropriate.

*   *   *

By heavily relying on case vignettes, I hope to highlight common practice themes and difficulties in treatment interaction in a wide variety of child and adolescent treatment scenarios.

By no means does this volume encompass every conceivable problem and diagnostic category. Rather, I hoped to indicate some of the ever-expanding scope and application of clinical work and to thereby reflect the nature of contemporary difficulties facing social workers working with children and adolescents. It is my fervent wish that my approach assist beginning therapists in their attempt to tackle the monumental dilemmas that face our clients, our profession of social work, and ultimately our society.

Part I

THE BEGINNING PHASE *of* TREATMENT

RELATIONAL THEORY
IN THE TREATMENT
OF CHILDREN

THE ANTECEDENTS
OF RELATIONAL THEORY

Ego Psychology

Ego psychology places emphasis on the ego and its relationship to the functioning of the individual and to the individual's relationship to the outside world.

Ego psychology is characterized by the view that people are born with the ability to function adaptively, that is, to flexibly cope with the external environment. The ego contains basic functions needed for adaptation to the environment. These functions include reality testing, judgment, regulation and control of the drives, thought processes, object relations, defensive functioning, and mastery competence (Goldstein, 1995).

Ego psychology evolved out of classical psychoanalytic theory. Freud's paper "The Ego and the Id" (1923) placed emphasis on the function of the ego and its place in the structure of the psyche. Later theorists—Hartmann, Anna Freud, Erikson, and many others—

developed concepts that expanded the ego. The ego mediates both one's internal life, through its need for preeminence over the id and superego, and one's connection to the external world, via its rational capacities for problem solving (Goldstein, 1995).

British Object Relations Theory

The psychoanalytic group known as the object relations theorists focused less on the adaptive components of the ego and more on the relationship of self to others (Flanagan, 1996). Object relations theorists such as Klein, Fairbairn, Winnicott, and Guntrip focused on how early external relationships are internalized and then brought to bear on both intrapsychic and interpersonal relations.

The British object relations group examined internalized object relations especially as they present in more pathological styles of relating. Fairbairn, in particular, based his theoretical contribution on his early work with traumatized children and adolescents. He was particularly struck by how abused children preferred to assume blame for their difficult relationships with their parents; they valued the relationship, no matter how abusive, over their own psychic and physical well-being. Fairbairn explained a child's allegiance to an abusive parent with the comment that the devil that we know is better than the one we don't know (Fairbairn, 1952). He examined how the psyche organizes around traumatic early relationships and seeks to use them as a model for interpersonal life. Developmental theorists such as Bowlby, Ainsworth, and Mahler added profound understanding to the importance of early relationships. Bowlby emphasized the profound importance of early attachment as central to human survival. He studied the psychological consequences of object loss in young children.

Mahler charted the phases of separation-individuation in toddlers. She observed that successful negotiation of the separation-individuation phases constituted an ability to have a healthy ego with the capacity for internal self-representation and object constancy. To have object constancy is to have a basically secure sense of self identity. Having achieved this, the toddler can also invest in important others, both in fantasy as object representations and in actual interpersonal relating.

While Mahler and other ego psychologists emphasized the movement of the infant from merger with mother to ultimate differentiation and independence, Bowlby, Ainsworth and others (in particular, the British object relations group) emphasized the course from nonattachment to attachment (Aron, 1996).

Self Psychology

Heinz Kohut developed self psychology out of classical psychoanalytic theory and ego psychology. Kohut believed that the individual has a core sense of self. Empathic mirroring by others is needed from earliest childhood in order for the individual to form a cohesive sense of self. Kohut conceived of a bipolar model for the psyche. He believed that the psyche contained polarities of grandiosity and idealization. Both grandiosity and idealization require others (self-objects) to provide affirmation in childhood. Early normal grandiosity in a young child must be mirrored or affirmed by parental figures. These figures are called grandiose self-objects, that is, objects whose empathic mirroring is necessary for the child's self-cohesion. Later on, self-objects can also be idealized, providing for the individual a sense of protection and ego ideals (Kohut, 1977). When these are adequately achieved, the individual can, as an adult, in turn mirror the needs of others in object relations.

The need for mirroring of grandiosity and idealization is seen as a developmental continuum throughout the life cycle. Developmental research from Daniel Stern, Joseph Lichtenberg, James Fosshage, Frank Lachmann, and Beatrice Beebe have added substantially to self psychology. This group has provided important infant research that challenges much of Margaret Mahler's work. Their research has yielded a picture of the infant that is active in seeking contact with the environment. They observed a greater use of the ego functions by infants than Mahler perceived (Beebe, 1993; Lichtenberg, 1989; Stern, 1985).

Lichtenberg conceived a model of the psyche based upon five motivational systems. These are the need for psychic regulation of physiological requirements; the need for attachment; the need for exploration and assertion; the need to respond adversely through antagonism and/or withdrawal; and the need for sensual pleasure and sexual stimulation. These systems are based on biological needs but become psychologically motivated as the result of early infant-caregiver relations (Lichtenberg, 1989; Aron, 1996).

CONCEPTS OF THE PSYCHE AND RELATIONAL THEORY

Ego psychology, object relations theory, self psychology, and the developmental theories are linked together in relational theory, providing a synthesized model for internal and interpersonal relationships. Throughout this book I will make references to various theoretical ideas from all of the above groups.

Relational theorists view the human psyche and its development as interactive by nature. Human beings are deeply social by nature and seek interaction with others. Stephen Mitchell has written that "minds seek contact, engagement with other minds" (1988). The earliest interpersonal interactions we experience shape the organization of our intrapsychic life and structure our interactions with others later on in life. Lewis Aron (1996) has suggested that "the relational approach is an attempt to bridge theories that have emphasized either internal object relations or external interpersonal relations, the intrapsychic or the interpersonal, constitutional factors or environmental factors, one-person psychology versus two-person psychologies" and has called the relational approach an eclectic theory that recognizes that relationships are "internal and external, real and imagined."

To apply this conceptual model to helping human beings is to combine an understanding of the subjectivity of the individual with an understanding of the intersubjective, contextual nature of relationships, including the client–therapist relationship. This model demands a careful understanding of the client's (and the therapist's) narrative. An understanding of the subjective meaning of narrative involves close attention to culture, social class, gender, and the linguistic distinctions that narrative can reveal. In this model the therapist must be aware of his or her own biases, theoretical beliefs, and the like before interpreting the client's.

UNDERSTANDING AND ANALYSIS

In the hermeneutic tradition, the therapist's narrative, principles, and beliefs are as important as the client's narrative in the mutual quest to create meaning. The judgments and assessments that a child therapist makes are a reflection of her own theoretical principles and personal beliefs. Our personal prejudices must be put outside to provide as accurate an empathic connection as possible to the child's experience. Relational theory invokes certain postmodernist precepts that social work has long held dear: understanding clients involves understanding their culture, race, social class, linguistic issues, and gender.

SELF-REGULATION

Self-regulation refers to the need of the individual to maintain a sense of cohesion not only by utilizing an internal system of differences and mechanisms but by balancing this in relation to others by way of interpersonal dynamics. For example, someone who feels insecure may ask for praise from others and to get praise may flatter others. This would be a means of maintaining a sense of self that counterbalances low self-esteem. Others can become involved in this process by offering the needed praise. The dynamic of excessive flattery may be a mode of behavior that has been learned early on as a way of negotiation with parents and other important, more powerful figures. In an example such as this, a child has learned to organize around the organizing principles of others and continues to do so later on in life as a way of dealing with underlying anxiety, both anxiety over a sense of self and anxiety over maintaining relationships.

This volume contains case examples of children whose psychodynamics were learned early on in life and maintained through their interactions with others.

Child and parent can activate and regulate each other. They can modify and affect each other in pursuit of attainment (Beebe & Lachman, 1988; Stern, 1985). They can create a mutually shared world of meaning, both symbolic and linguistic, about personal and external experiences.

The therapist's engagement in treatment with a client also reflects this early dyadic experience. Therapists, however, must be active participants in the therapeutic adventure. In child treatment, they must provide empathic connection so that they can experience the child's perceptions of self and the world. This can be done from the perspective of the therapist *in the relationship with the child.* Fosshage (1994) terms this the "other-centered listening perspective." Listening and experiencing are shaped by the subjectivity of the therapist, that is, by the therapist's theoretical orientation, individuality, history, and so on. Fosshage suggests that however we view a patient (e.g., as controlling, offensive, or humorous), we are hearing and experiencing the patient as the other within the therapeutic relationship, the "other-centered perspective." The therapist is used for self-regulatory purposes but is only one aspect of the dimension of relatedness (Stolorow, 1986).

CLINICAL SOCIAL WORK AND RELATIONAL THEORY

In many respects, clinical social work has often utilized common principles with relational theory. The primary importance of respect for the client's autonomy has been a long-held social work value. This respect for the client's autonomy has evolved into a respect for difference and an understanding that race, culture, religious belief, gender, social class, and sexual orientation influence not only one's perception of the outside world but also one's experience of and expectation of response from the outside world.

Adult clients describe routine experiences of abusive treatment on the basis of race, sexual orientation, physical disability, and so on. Children will also describe such experiences if the therapist can be nondefensive and open to hearing about cruelty and unfairness in the world.

SOCIAL CONSTRUCTIVISM, PSYCHOTHERAPY, AND CHILDREN

A social constructivist approach to treatment encompasses a variety of theoretical concepts necessary for understanding contemporary life. In application to clients and psychotherapy, a constructivist approach enhances the therapist's understanding of the very real stressors and differences that clients bring to the therapeutic experience. The realities of race, social conditions, and their accompanying stressors are all important elements that construct identity.

A constructivist approach targets the following areas for intervention: the personal narrative of the client—which reflects the client's sense of meaning, perception of events, belief systems, and system of self-organization—and the systems within which the client must function, including developmental stage. All these influence the client's construction of experience and action (McNamee, 1992).

Thinking is in itself a product of the time and place one inhabits. It is therefore a highly subjective reflection of one's view of reality.

The subjectivity of perspective is abundantly apparent in childhood and adolescence. Anyone who has ever argued with a child (or an adolescent) is struck by the persistence with which children adhere to their own perspective of reality and sense of justice, as opposed to what may actually have occurred (from the adult's perspective).

Knowledge can be validated by an understanding and acknowledgment of diverse interpretations and by an examination of its consistency with existing structures by knowledgeable observers within that system. For example, an adolescent living in the inner city may seem unduly suspicious or even paranoid about being the target of potentially destructive, hostile activity from other adolescents. This response may seem excessive in relationships outside the adolescent's familiar world, but it may be quite appropriate even on a daily basis in his community.

Joe, a former gang member, described being identified by an unknown rival gang member while both attended a job training camp. Joe was subsequently viciously assaulted by his rival and others. Rather than stay at camp, Joe decided to return home. His therapist understood the reality of Joe's sense of fear even though curtailment of the camp experience was a sad loss of opportunity for him. They discussed how he might disguise his gang affiliation in the future and worked toward an alternative plan.

Our internal world stays with us despite the actual geographical location we may inhabit. In understanding Joe's dilemma, the social worker had to acknowledge the reality of his life experiences and the very real potential that existed for future conflict. While assisting Joe in being more circumspect and self-protective in the future, she also had empathy for his internal terrors of the outside world.

Anna Freud, Sandler, et al. (1980) described the different types of transference that children and adolescents might have during therapy. These included transferences of current and past relationships and ways of relating, of the therapist as object for externalization and internalization of conflicts, and of the therapist as "real" object. S. Warshaw (1992) suggests that this real object can be a source of identification or an auxiliary ego and that the child therapist creates for the child the experience of being known and heard. As a result, the therapist can "notice the unnoticeable" and "validate the awful realities" of the important fissures previously not validated in the child's life. The interpersonal perspective and real experiences that are processed at each developmental level are central to understanding the triggers and stimulants of pathology (Warshaw, 1992).

The therapist is both a new and an old object to a child (Altman, 1992; Mishne, 1993). In classical psychoanalysis the transference relationship was separated conceptually from the "real" relationship (Mishne, 1993). In the relational perspective, the transference is regarded as reflecting other real relationships and the subjective and intersubjective modes of reality required by them.

CHAPTER 2

RELATIONAL THEORY
IN THE TREATMENT
OF ADOLESCENTS

THE HERO OF THE
TWENTIETH CENTURY

The social historian Philippe Aries described the modern-day adolescent as "the hero of the twentieth century," a descendant of Siegfried, the adolescent hero of Teutonic mythology, as a culturally invented prototype. Siegfried's beauty, purity, idealism, and bravery made him the arch idealized romantic figure for adolescent prototypes to come.

Western society has made adolescence an enviable phase to members of all other generations. Indeed, life depicted in the myth of adolescence is enviable (and unattainable as an ideal) to adolescents themselves.

EGO PSYCHOLOGY AND EARLY THEORISTS OF ADOLESCENCE

Anna Freud, Erik Erikson, Peter Blos, and August Aichhorn wrote seminal psychoanalytic works on adolescence. They wrote from the perspective of classical theory, ego psychology, and, later, the developmental research of Margaret Mahler. They viewed adolescence as a time of normal disruption due to the stress of separation (the "second separation-individuation," according to Blos); to puberty and genital sexuality; and to the demands of forming a viable identity, including the intrapsychic "selective repudiations and identifications" posited by Erikson. Although the early theorists' work was invaluable to an understanding of adolescence, psychoanalysis has long needed to readdress its concept of this stage of life.

EGO PSYCHOLOGY AND CHILD THERAPY

The early ego psychologists who worked with children focused on sustaining a supportive and positive connection to the child, one that could bolster the child's ego. This meant being encouraging of the child's utilization of ego functions and defenses. The ego functions, which include reality testing, judgment, and object relations as well as the primary adaptive ego functions of memory, intelligence, and choice of action (motility), assist in a flexible adaptation to the daily demands of everyday life. The ego fosters optimal functioning; via secondary process thinking (i.e., rational, reality-oriented, grammatical thinking), it promotes connectedness to reality, others, and the outside world.

The ego psychologists used treatment to help their clients repress id impulses (primitive and usually aggressive in nature). This method continues to work very well with children whose problems are neurotic in nature, that is, children who have enough basic psychological structure to be able to learn to repress unconscious id impulses. Repression is a defense that is central to neurotics. However, children (and adults) who have not successfully attained object constancy utilize the primary defense of splitting. Splitting refers to both ego and object and implies ego weakness and a lack of ability to integrate good and bad aspects of the self and others into a basically positive sense of self. It is only when object constancy is achieved that one can have basic trust in others. When the ego is strong, lower defenses such as splitting, projection, denial, and grandiosity can be tempered by object constancy, judgment, and higher-level defenses.

Anna Freud believed that the child therapist should not attempt to interpret id impulses. Rather, the therapist should attempt to maintain a positive transference with the child. The early child therapists—Anna Freud, Erick Erikson, and Peter Blos, among others—were often teachers of children. As analysts of children, they presented themselves as therapist-educators who fostered their young clients' connectedness to the outside world (Warsaw, 1992). Therapy was considered a reeducation (as Freud initially suggested).

In post–World War II America, as elsewhere, therapists in child guidance settings began routinely to see children whose lack of internal structure was pronounced. Often, these children and their families were being subjected to grave social stressors; racism, the stress of immigration, poverty, and lack of social support all contributed to debilitating the families' psychological, emotional, and economic capacities. The children in these severely stressed families often resorted to delinquent activities as a result of too little formal structure in the environment and lack of limit setting. Family violence resulted in physical and sexual abuse of children. Instead of physical violence, some children experienced denigration, derision, and scapegoating in the home.

These problems often resulted in a lack of internal structure in children. Ego weakness in such children is profound, with little superego except for its most ruthless, self-punishing aspects. Object constancy is limited, and the capacity for object relations of these children is severely deficient. In these cases, children often repel attempts to help them. They view adults in particular with suspicion and mistrust. Adults in helping professions who attempt to offer or create a positive relationship with such children are often met with derision and maltreatment themselves.

The newer ideas of attachment theory, object relations theory, and self psychology helped to illuminate this type of pathology. The work of researchers and theorists such as Bowlby, Klein, Fairbairn, Winnicott, Kohut, and Stern enabled child therapists to examine child pathology in a different light. These theorists have made substantial contributions to an understanding of the human condition that are especially relevant to an examination of the problems of adolescence.

By the use of projection, children with psychological deficits experience others as relating to them like abusive or abandoning parental figures. Their behavior (toward themselves and others) can be seen as a continuation of their early relationships, now structured into their sense of self. Their behavior toward others and their experience of self are attempts to maintain connectedness in the only way they know. In these cases an understanding of the child's inability to relate positively to others is imperative. The therapist needs to work with the child to create an internal structure out of the treatment relationship.

Object relations theorists (in particular, Melanie Klein) extended and elaborated upon the defense mechanisms to include the so-called lower defenses: grandiosity, denial, primitive devaluation and idealization, projection, and projective identification. These are the defenses that are heavily utilized by clients who are fixated in a borderline structure, that is, fixated in the rapprochement subphase, which prohibits object constancy from being achieved (Goldstein, 1995).

"THE BAD, EXCITING OBJECT" IN ADOLESCENCE

Fairbairn developed his concept of the moral defense from his work with delinquent adolescents. He found that abused children and adolescents cling to the notion that it is they themselves who are "bad," even when there is evidence that their parents are severely abusive. Rather than be separated from their parents, they choose instead to conceive of themselves as having failed. In a sense, this is a very moral defense, because the child assumes responsibility for a relationship gone awry, as opposed to simply abandoning the relationship altogether. The "bad, exciting object" is located in the self and also in object relations in attachment to certain kinds of relationships. These relationships can be real in their destructiveness or imagined (by way of projection) or created (by way of projective identification). Excitement (and a sense of being alive) is achieved by the child by the excitation of a hope. The hope is that love will finally be achieved and the self redeemed. In earlier classical conceptualizations this would have been described as repetition compulsion; that is, repeating until one wins or gets it right.

Adolescents are especially conscious of what is exciting and what is bad. In their minds, Fairbairn suggested, it is better to be seen as bad than to be seen as a nonentity, that is, to not exist at all. In adolescence, as in adult preoedipal conditions, the feeling and sense of danger often enables one to feel that one is at least alive, that one is real. The excessive pathologies of adolescence—attraction to violence, danger, and hazardous sexuality; self-mutilation—are all means of feeling alive and denying deadness even when actual death is gambled with. Perilous relationships may encourage this, but an adolescent with a sense of self as bad and exciting will unerringly gravitate toward the impossible and destructive.

Case Example: Midphase Treatment of a Delinquent Boy

Tom, a young adolescent, well known to the police, had been nearly arrested on a number of occasions. During a recent therapy session, he described a car chase he had been involved in to his therapist: He had successfully managed to steal a car, but then he spied a nearby police car and immediately stepped on the gas pedal. This provoked a police chase. In Tom's community, the police were known to be violently abusive to offenders. By provoking them, he made the potential of abuse that much greater. He somehow managed to avoid capture, but his car left tire tracks on the street. Tom expressed a wish that his therapist see them; unconsciously, he wanted his therapist to provide a mirroring self-object to his grandiose, omnipotent fantasy of triumphing over the police (as well as over potential homicide or suicide).

Underlying the adolescent's dangerous activities is a wish to commit suicide. Even when homicide is the overt intent, suicide is equally a potential reality, because one can always be killed in the process.

Analysis and Intervention

The therapist explored Tom's sense of excitation, first over stealing the car and then over the subsequent car chase. This exploration had to be done carefully, that is, without expressing voyeurism or approval over the elaborately described episode. The therapist had to be aware of his own need for excitation and also of his envy of the boy's daring and daredevil qualities. His affect during this therapy session had to be serious but neutral (to allow for the boy's narrative to continue). The challenge was to avoid starting a lecture on danger too soon, thereby cutting off dialogue with the client.

The therapist linked Tom's sense of excitation with a feeling of needing to exist and with how dead Tom often in fact felt. He commented that Tom's previous brushes with the police meant that one more arrest would undoubtedly put him in incarceration. He suggested (based on earlier historical reports from Tom) that Tom might need to see himself as bad and exciting and therefore as similar to his parents, who were frustrating and neglectful (therefore, bad and exciting). By provoking the perceived dangerous, abusive police into a very real engagement (i.e., with projection toward the police provoking projective identification), Tom succeeded in exciting their attention and getting them to perceive him as bad. The therapist refused to witness the tire tracks, opting instead to listen to Tom describe them. If the therapist had actually viewed the tracks, he would have been unwittingly encouraging Tom, by admiring his impressive risk taking, to continue to risk killing himself.

David Celani (1992) has examined the relationship of delinquent boys to their fathers. He found that the fathers were often physically abusive, the boys could not express their rage and aggression toward the father because they also were dependent on him. They could not bear to lose the father because they had become so identified with him. To lose the gratification provided by the father's exciting qualities or to become disenchanted with him would be to lose oneself. This dynamic often occurred in combination with a mother who was also unavailable and unprotective, making the son's need to idealize the father all the more critical.

In their lack of differentiation between self and parent, adolescents often feel a sense of shame over a parent's abusiveness and lack of nurturing. Caught in a bad-object tie, these adolescents assume the burden of shame themselves.

Case Example: The Acting Out of a Conflict of Dependency

Tina, an adolescent girl living in a New York City ghetto, was the child of a Latina mother and an Italian father. The father never lived with the family and was neglectful and often absent. Tina was raised principally in her mother's culture. She was the girlfriend of a young Italian gang leader; he and his peers were continually involved in racial and ethnic wars with other gangs. Tina had recently begun to flirt with the Hispanic leader of a rival gang. When friends of her Italian boyfriend informed him of the growing friendship, he and the rival gang leader decided to fight each other (along with their gangs). Tina excitedly described the planned fight to her therapist. Interestingly, she opted to show up for her therapy appointing rather than accompany one gang leader or the other to the battle.

Tina clearly saw herself as the dangerous and exciting object of desire. She seemed to have little regard for the danger the gang members placed themselves in by fighting over her. She displayed an affective exhilaration as she described the lengths to which they might go to have her. She seemed to have no conscious sense that the leaders and their gangs might in fact become abusive of her. Nevertheless, some unconscious awareness of this may have been the reason she wisely opted to attend her therapy appointment rather than the scene of conflict. In a sense, Tina saw herself only as the possession of either boy, more of a thing or an ornament than a person. Fundamental in bad-object ties is a lack of differentiation that leaves one with a sense of the self as a part object, that is, as a person who is incomplete (e.g., Tina saw herself only as an object of desire). Being free to choose her potential boyfriends (or choosing none at all) would be, for Tina, to feel that she didn't exist. Indifference, indecision, or lack of relationships would lead her to feel nonexistent and fundamentally abandoned and unwanted.

Tina saw both boys as part object relationships as well. They were only meaningful to her as phallic signifiers or as willing but symbolic participants in a drama that made her feel valued at the expense of their own safety. They enacted the conflict between mother and father that had become internalized in Tina; even better, their behavior gave her a chance to feel alive and very much wanted by both.

Analysis and Intervention

Tina's therapist had to act quickly to avert the gang war. She pointed out the crisis and danger at hand. Because she had a relationship with the girl, the therapist could demand that Tina phone her boyfriend immediately to end the battle—which Tina was able to do. After being assured that the potential for violence had subsided (and after alerting other authorities to the possibility of gang warfare), the therapist then began to point out the conflict in Tina. She described how and why this enactment was so compelling to her despite the danger that she had put herself in. Here, dependence on an abandoning parent was transferred to a boyfriend. When an adolescent's exciting, bad relationship is finally understood as dependent and infantile, a large degree of excitation can be removed. The adolescent's dependency can then shift to the therapist, allowing therapist and client to address it directly in their relationship.

DEPRESSION, THE BAD, EXCITING OBJECT, AND THE INTRAPSYCHIC VENDETTA

Not all adolescents act out the bad, exciting object in sensational dramas. This concept can also be seen in depression.

Adolescents from immigrant families and families that have been oppressed by racism and poverty often have to function as "parentified" children (i.e., pretend adults who act in a parental style, caregiving for the family's benefit). This can be true of the children of substance abusers as well. We are all culturally inscribed in society by birth in terms of race, gender, economic class, and so on (Irvine, 1991; Neimery, 1995). With families who have consistently experienced unfairness and tragedy, however, the burden of vindication often falls upon the children. This can be demonstrated as a wish to triumph over adversity to vindicate one's family. However, this wish to triumph may involve setting up intolerably high standards for oneself or wishing to acquire outlandish and unreasonable fame and fortune. As we can see in every part of the world today, vindication is often enacted as a literal vendetta in the endless tribal, racial, and ethnic wars whose origins go back centuries.

The intrapsychic vendetta, as I have termed it, is an introjection characterized by excessive guilt. Guilt stands for a tie of loyalty to an important object relationship (Fairbairn, 1943). In the fantasy of vindication, it is as if the act of winning serves to finally impress an important observer, who will approve and be gratified and therefore loving in return. Over it, the therapist must become an important witness to this fantasy as well. The fantasy that has been dyadic is then triadic.

The bad, exciting object in depression can take the following forms: feeling overwhelmed; feeling guilt for not living up to the excessively high standards set by the ego ideal; feeling unwanted or unloved by family, teachers, and peers; feeling ugly and boring to others (Fairbairn, 1941, 1943, 1954).

For adolescents of oppressed minority groups, the sense of shame in not reflecting a dominant society's values can extend to shame and embarrassment over their family or their race or ethnicity.

Case Example: Midphase Treatment Use of the Model Scene

Maia, fourteen years old, was the eldest child of Asian immigrant parents. Maia was born in America. Her parents arrived several years prior to her birth. Maia's family was extremely poor. Both parents were sporadically employed in jobs far below the educational level they had achieved in their country of origin. The family put a high premium on their daughter's intellectual ability. Although it was difficult for them to do so, they chose to continue living in the city because of Maia's acceptance to a very high-pressured, academically rigorous high school.

Maia functioned as a parentified child in every sense. She translated for her parents, supervised younger siblings, worried over expenditures (especially when they seemed to her to be frivolous), and so on. When her mother had to be hospitalized for a very serious suicide attempt (the most recent of many such attempts), the young girl was terrified and finally requested help from her school guidance counselor.

Maia was able to see her therapist very positively as a source of help. She described an intense sense of shame because her grades were barely average (not surprising given the amount of stress she was under). Maia's therapist had the distinct sense of a child frantically running from one adult to another in search of help—a model scene.

The Model Scene

The model scene (Lichtenberg, 1989) utilizes a construct by patient and therapist that (1) expresses an important communication about the patient's life, (2) signifies an important developmental experience, and (3) expresses either by fantasy or pathological belief the significance of some past experience. Maia's sense of shame over her poor grades shifted into an inability to complete her work. Because of the severity of the family pathology, the therapist had given her young client her home phone number. The girl frequently called in panic over her school assignments. The therapist had first to ascertain that things were relatively stable at home; then she attempted to calm her client and to reassure that they could discuss her problems more fully in a therapy session.

Maia held herself to impossible standards. In reality, she was performing heroically under great duress. Through her transference to her social worker, she attempted to live up to the therapist as an ego ideal with high standards; it was as if Maia had to please the social worker, just as she had tried to please her parents with dazzling accomplishments.

The therapist didn't disparage Maia's standards as being too high. Maia needed these goals, not only as a defensive function but also as a connection to her parents and their Confucian ideals of study and achievement. To encourage Maia to adopt more realistic standards, the therapist had to function as an idealized self-object, because she was needed in this capacity. The therapist was often described by her client as the kind of strong, intellectual woman she wished her mother could be and that she herself wished to be. It was important for Maia to be able to express her feelings of dependency on her therapist, as feelings of shame are often related to the humiliation of feeling dependent on others.

Later on in treatment, the therapist was able to address Maia's wish to vindicate her parents from their humiliating situation in America. This need for vindication placed a difficult burden on the girl but also gave her the impetus to realize her own considerable potential. In therapy Maia learned that having to achieve for the sole purpose of pleasing others had kept her angry and unable to complete her schoolwork.

SELF PSYCHOLOGY AND ADOLESCENCE

Another important view of shame comes from Heinz Kohut's model of self psychology. The self psychological view emphasizes the symptom of shame as emanating from the normal exhibitionistic desires of earliest childhood. When very young children are consistently made to feel humiliation over their early attempts to seek attention or display their abilities, even simply by talking or asking for help, a pervasive sense of shame (and, ultimately, poor self-esteem) is the result. Feelings of hopelessness and despair are the ultimate outcomes of depression (Kohut, 1987). A chronic sense of shame can be the result of not living up to excessively high standards demanded by the superego. Pervasive shame can also result from feeling embarrassed and humiliated by early infantile grandiose wishes and demonstrations. For example, a child who is constantly told to be seen and not heard may feel shame over wishes to express oneself and be highly sensitive to criticism of behavior. Over time this sense of shame will weaken self-esteem and add to feelings of hopelessness.

Adolescents are at particular risk for suicidal ideation. When a family member, friend, or significant other has died, the potential for suicide is especially great. Humiliation over perceived loss (e.g., failure in school activities or the breakup of a relationship) is also a source of concern to the therapist of adolescents. The anniversary dates of losses or other events are also important to bear in mind.

Self psychology is an extremely relevant model for those who study adolescence. In this model two polarities are believed to be required for a sufficiency of psychic equilibrium. The "grandiose self" is the earliest aspect of self requiring mirroring from important parental self-objects. Grandiose self-objects provide mirroring that is empathic. In early childhood a grandiose self-object provides appropriate admiration and encouragement. This in turn enables the young child to become "self-regulating," that is, enables the child to develop the ability to become self-soothing later on. The child also develops a cohesive "nuclear self." In time the child who receives an adequate sufficiency of the grandiose self will be able to provide mirroring to others in object relationships.

The second polarity is that of the "idealizing self." This part of the self seeks to look to others in admiration and for a sense of protection and calm. This seeking can take the form of admiration for the qualities and abilities of parental figures, peers, teachers, therapists, and famous figures in popular culture. The objects of idealization by adolescents who have been seriously deprived can be alarming: ominous, menacing figures whose grandiosity can jeopardize the safety and sanity of others (e.g., drug pushers, criminals, etc.).

The real object who is idealized provides the adolescent with an idealized self-object relationship. Therapists who work with adolescents are frequently recipients of an idealized self-object transference. By allowing this as long as it is needed, therapists provide patients with the potential for self-regulation and achievement in that they not only mirror back to their patients the need for someone who can provide safety and protection but also represent standards and goals to be met. It is equally important for therapists to let patients give up the need for idealization when they are ready to do so. There is a difference between idealization (which is defensive in nature) and admiration, which is based less on illusion and more on valuing real qualities. In the previous case examples, the therapists served alternating functions as grandiose and idealized self-objects.

ACTION AND ACTING OUT

One of the more delicate skills required in assessing an adolescent is the ability to distinguish between action and acting out. Often adolescents choose a course of action that may be less than ideal because they are experimenting with choices involving autonomy and, more specifically, the use of judgment. Kohut suggested that a choice of action involves utilizing the ego functions. The ego functions of judgment, reality testing, object relations, regulation of drives and impulses, and mastery competence are all called into play in the formulation of a course of action. Action is also concerned with knowledge of the consequences of an act (Kohut, 1987).

When the ego functions manifest gross impairments and reality testing is eroded, thought is dominated on the extreme end by delusional thinking, hallucinations, and distortions of perception. Freud (1914) defined acting out as a means of repeating the unconscious past during the course of analytic work. Occasionally, acting out is demonstrated in the treatment relationship itself. Fenichel conceptualized acting out as unconsciously relieving tension or warding off guilt over instinctual impulses. He also pointed to the presence of trauma in producing repetition compulsion. Greenacre (1952), following Fenichel's definition of acting out, added the following to the list of possible causes: difficulty in accepting current reality because of specific problems in real life, a persistence of earlier disturbing memories, and "a special emphasis on visual sensitizing" (with derivatives of exhibitionism, voyeurism, and an unconscious belief in the magic of action).

Case Example

Jim, an engaging sixteen-year-old, had been in a series of mishaps with police and school authorities. One of his best friends, Rob, engineered a burglary. However, Jim was not in any way involved; in fact, on the night of the burglary he was with his girlfriend and her family. Nonetheless, Jim was confronted by police and charged with the crime. He strongly felt that he must not betray his friend, despite the availability of responsible and ready witnesses to attest to his lack of involvement in the burglary. Jim also knew that given his previous history of delinquent activity he might be treated severely by the court.

Analysis and Intervention

Jim's social worker was empathic in understanding the adolescent's predicament and admiring of his loyalty to his friend. He pointed out that Jim was being a better friend to Rob than Rob was to him, that Rob was not employing the same standard of behavior. Given the gravity of charges that awaited Jim, Rob's selfish behavior was especially disturbing. Jim nonetheless remained adamant about proving his loyalty to Rob.

The therapist encouraged Jim to share his thoughts with him. Jim told him how he had been reading a novel about a boy who is the son of a criminal. The boy in the novel makes a choice to renounce his father's lifestyle and lead a law-biding life. Jim was deeply impressed by the story. He said that he often felt that he too could be a social worker, like his therapist, and that he would really know how to help kids. But he said that if it meant renouncing his father, who was often involved in illegal activities, he would never do so. All the therapist could do (at this juncture) was to point out the conflict between the goals Jim had expressed in therapy and his attachment to his father. He reflected that Jim seemed to feel that loyalty involved an all-or-nothing response and that he, Jim, could have an identity made up of the better parts of his father, aspects of his therapist, and his own intrinsic abilities and talents.

This case example is one of acting out. On the surface, Jim's decision may appear to be a choice of action based on the ego functions; however, there is a powerful unconscious motive at work in his situation. Jim is clearly choosing to be identified as a criminal (like his father), in part out of loyalty but also out of guilt. In Jim's mind, to declare his innocence might be to separate himself from his father, an act of renunciation that would be fraught with guilt for him. Using the defense of repetition compulsion, he unconsciously is reenacting his conflictual relationship with his father.

Case Example

Jenny, a lively sixteen-year-old, described going to parties on the weekend that caused her therapist some concern. Jenny called these parties "keg parties" and described them as being dominated by unlimited beer and unchaperoned. Typically, fights would break out among the boys after midnight when they were drunk. The police would then be called.

The therapist knew that to forbid these parties would be a fruitless task. Instead, she asked Jenny if she knew how to protect herself in such situations. Jenny described always going to the parties with at least one male or female friend. They would agree in advance to leave the party together; however, Jenny always brought taxi fare in case she had to return home alone. She went on to say that she knew it was time to leave when the first fight broke out, since this typically meant that more fights would follow and that the police would be called.

Analysis and Intervention

The therapist carefully outlined with Jenny all of the possible difficult scenarios evolving out of a keg party. Together they figured out optimal strategies to deal with each situation.

Jenny's behavior can be seen as a choice of action on her part. Even though she felt compelled to attend these less than desirable parties, it was clear that Jenny did not overindulge in drinking herself. She did, however, voice trust in her therapist's wisdom and said that she knew when it was time to ask her for help. She would often run a problem by her parents or friends first; if their answers were somehow unsatisfactory, she would then ask her therapist. It was important for Jenny to feel competence in her ability to problem-solve first on her own, utilizing her own resources, even though she ultimately turned to her therapist when the former sources were inadequate.

Adolescents clearly need to experiment with making choices and with utilizing their own judgment and choice of action. This may mean making occasional mistakes or choosing a dubious course of action as the demand for autonomous functioning and the need for differentiation from parental figures increase. The therapist can help adolescent clients achieve autonomy by being cognizant of their need to master issues of judgment, action, and the consequences of an act.

CHAPTER 3

DIAGNOSTIC ASSESSMENT OF CHILDREN

THE FIRST INTERVIEW WITH A CHILD

The first therapy session sets the tone for both child and adult clients. This session can be a model of what treatment will be: discussion and sharing of ideas, exploration, and assistance.

In the first session of child therapy, it is advisable to meet with both the child and the family, if at all possible. I begin the session by setting a tone that is warm and friendly so that my clients, whether children or adults, will feel less frightened or intimidated by the meeting. Excessive formality or rigidity is off-putting to new clients. The social worker should be seen as a source of help in problem solving and as a trustworthy, receptive, reliable person who can help them feel comfortable enough to express their feelings. If the parents appear very formal, the therapist needs to be attuned and sensitive to this.

I begin the session by asking the child and family if they know why they are here. If the child does not know or is under a misunderstanding about the nature of the visit, I ask the parents (or guardians) to give the reason for the visit. If the explanation is inadequate, I then explain the purpose of the session myself. For example: "Tommy, I understand that you were having some trouble at school. Is that correct? Can you tell me about it?" I then ask when the problem seemed to begin, what incidents may have occurred as precipitants, and how the family understands the problem.

At this point, I explain how the process of therapy works. I begin by saying to the child and the parents that this is a place where children can talk about problems they have been having. I often tell the child that other children have described this as a place where they can talk about things that worry them or that they are thinking about. I point out that there are toys and games here because children can't always talk like adults can and that we can play and talk as well. This is important for parents to hear, as they may perceive play therapy as trivial or as an attempt to placate the child.

I then ask if I may talk to the child alone. If this is agreeable to all, I ask the parents to leave, and I let the child know that family members will be nearby, in the waiting area. If separation seems too threatening, then I continue on in a family therapy format.

When the child is alone, I suggest that he look around, explore the room, examine the toys, and so on. I find paper and colored markers and ask the child if he would draw me a picture of his family and of his home. Children of separated or divorced parents or of blended families often ask, "Which family?" I suggest they draw the whole family in any way they like. (Some children make one picture of themselves and their parents, siblings, and extended family members; others make many pictures, always including themselves as part of the picture.)

The family drawing is a very useful diagnostic tool, and it is also a source of dynamic information. For example, if certain family members are estranged from others and require separate pictures or if the child finds it too difficult to draw certain family members, then important information about family conflicts has been disclosed. I ask the child to tell me a story about what the family members are doing in the picture. I also ask the child to elaborate further (if possible) by asking a question that is a hypothesis. For example: "It is really hard on kids if Mommy and Daddy won't speak to each other. What is that like for you?" The open-ended nature of this question enables the child to fill in information that illuminates the family's problems and that can potentially be used for exploration when the adults become involved in the therapy.

I suggest that therapists bear in mind the style of housing in a child's community when assessing a child's drawing of her home. For example, in California the entrance to an apartment house is often through the garage, which is usually below the apartment building. For the child who lives in an area where this is not the case, a drawing showing entry into the home through the basement might take on a different significance.

In viewing a child's drawing of family members, I compare the height of the child to that of the adults. A child who is drawn as the same height as the adults may see herself as "parentified," that is, as acting as a parent to the adults in the family; the child might also be using the defense of grandiosity, with her drawing expressing her wish to diminish the authority of the adults. I would ask the child, "How come the adults are the same size as you?" This question should be asked in a curious, as opposed to a confrontational, tone to encourage the child to explore this paradox further.

If the child refuses to leave the pictures behind when the session ends, I ask if we could make copies because I would like to think about these before our next session.

I also ask the child to pick three wishes: "If you could have three wishes, what would they be?" The wishes are often telling of deeper wishes still. Again, I encourage the child to describe these further (by asking, for example, what would it mean if the wishes were granted). Other topics to ask about and to explore are the child's interests, friends, school, teachers, and hobbies. I ask children what the best experience of their life was and what the worst was. I also ask if they remember any dreams, good or bad.

At this point, I ask children if anything bad has ever happened to them or is happening to them right now. I ask if anyone at home or elsewhere is doing anything hurtful to them or anything that makes them feel uncomfortable. Obviously, these questions are designed to explore physical, emotional, and sexual abuse. The less experienced social worker may have to practice these questions, as they clearly are the hardest to ask.

I also ask children if there is anything they would like me to help them with or talk to their parents or teachers about. This at least suggests the advocacy role that therapists can play for children. Finally, I ask children if there is anything else they would like to tell me, and I assure them that if they think of something during the week, they can tell me about it next time. (In the second session, I often ask children and adolescents if they had any thoughts about our last session.) This provides a sense of continuity to the therapy sessions. If the child has had any unconscious associations or reactions to things we talked about in the first session, this question encourages discussion.

CHAPTER 4

DIAGNOSTIC ASSESSMENT OF ADOLESCENTS

When meeting with an adolescent for the first therapy session, I prefer to start with the adolescent alone, if at all possible. This is particularly important if treatment has failed in the past. Many adolescents do not want to be present in an initial family session, especially if the parental figures are angry. I also believe that adolescents should not be treated as children or as appendages of their family. It can be humiliating to adolescents to hear a parent recount a list of grievances against them.

I begin the session similarly to a child session by asking adolescent clients if they know why they are here. I ask what their life experience is like. One way to explore this is to ask about what a typical day is like. I pay careful attention to the narrative: Is the content logical and clear, or is a thought disorder present? If the latter hypothesis is supported, I explain that I would like to ask what may seem like funny questions. Then I ask questions like the following: Do you ever see anything that isn't there? Do your eyes ever play tricks on you? Do you ever hear any voices that you are not sure are there? Become aware of peculiar smells or feelings? What is the weirdest experience you've ever had?

The therapist may have a working diagnosis/hypothesis in mind based on the history that has been provided. For example, if an adolescent is highly active, the therapist may want to consider the possible nature of the underlying cause: Attention-Deficit/Hyperactivity Disorder, a manic-like episode to cover or mask depression and loss, substance abuse, and so on. A cluster of symptoms will often suggest the diagnosis.

In the diagnostic assessment of children or adolescents, the following factors need to be ruled out: developmental delay, organic deficits, thought disorder, conflict and anxiety, psychosomatic disorder (this diagnosis requires a physician's report), mental retardation (requires psychological testing), reactive disorder, and genetically predisposed disorder (family history may suggest this). Headaches need to be checked by a physician and/or dentist (and possibly by neurological examination) to rule out brain tumors, organic disorders, and dental disease.

If the child or adolescent appears to blank out momentarily in school, at home, or in the office, the therapist should pursue a neurological assessment for seizure disorders. (One adolescent with seizure disorder reported a routine absentmindedness that resulted in her being burned by excessively hot water in the shower when she reportedly "blanked out.")

Outside of organic disorders, a history of accidents and injuries may point to suicidal ideation. If a child or adolescent client describes wishing to kill herself, I would ask if she has a plan. If the plan is easily implemented, a psychiatric interview is mandated to consider hospitalization. In some states, certain social workers are allowed to make that decision, but typically a physician must make the ultimate decision whether or not to hospitalize.

Symptoms like delicate cutting (usually of arms or other concealable body parts), running away, substance abuse, and self-destructive or occasional antisocial behavior can point to posttramatic stress disorder (from physical or sexual abuse). If acting out episodes follow a pattern, I ask about important anniversaries, especially regarding losses of family members or friends. For example, one twelve-year-old client described having a serious accident every year in the spring. He was able to trace this back to the spring when his mother left home.

Parents who have died or who are rejecting, abandoning, or psychotic may be unconsciously commemorated by the child or adolescent in episodes of acting out, especially if these occur at certain times of the year.

Acting out is essentially an invented concept of current usage. Initially, Freud used the phrase to refer to unconscious repetitions of themes or issues in the transference. Today, the phrase is often used to describe what the therapist considers to be unconventional or disturbed behavior. As a rule of thumb, it is best to think about young clients' behavior in terms of how much danger or risk they are placing themselves in. How self-destructive is the behavior? How else is it manifested in daily life or in relationships?

ISSUES OF TECHNIQUE

In their first session, I ask adolescents how they see the problem or precipitant. (This may be very different from the parent's view.) If the adolescent talks or asks a question in the third person (e.g., "Can a person get pregnant from kissing?"), I answer in the third person. This sort of distancing may be the adolescent's way of testing the trustworthiness of the therapist. Hostility from the client also may be a test of the therapist or a defense against anxiety. It is often a displacement of rage against a parent. The therapist can try asking about a client's hostility: "You seem really angry at something. Can I help you with it?"

I prefer not to allow silences to go on too long, so as to prevent power/control issues from erupting. If necessary, I offer a game or task that the adolescent and I can do jointly.

It is important to utilize flexibility with adolescents. It is best not to be rigid about when the session ends: be guided by the comfort of the child/adolescent.

Confidentiality cannot be kept in the assessment phase. It is important to be clear about this to the client. For example, any court-referred case may require disclosure of the assessment content to court officials.

At the end of the assessment interview, it is a good idea to give some kind of conceptualized hypothesis to an adolescent client. For example: "It sounds as if you have struggled with things that have happened to you for a long time now, and you have dealt with this as best as you could. But I wonder if there are times when you need to start to think more about protecting yourself better. Maybe we could work on this together."

I offer any treatment goal as something that the client can work on with me, as something that we can *both* be active in developing together. I also tell adolescents and their parents that in the end the adolescents themselves will determine how their life goes, that I can offer help that they can use—or not, as they wish. I also tell them that what I say isn't written in stone; if they disagree with what I suggest, I need them to tell me.

Therapy will only work for clients if it really makes sense to them.

DEVELOPMENTAL HISTORY

The developmental history should ideally be done with both parents present. I begin by telling the parents that they know their child better than I do and that I will need their assistance throughout treatment.

This solicitation for assistance is important to parents who may feel threatened by a therapist, either in terms of feeling criticized or out of fear of somehow being pushed out of their child's life (especially if the child's attachment to the therapist is considerable).

Outline for Developmental History

FOR EXPLORATION:

1. Parents' relationship:

   Begin by asking about the parents' relationship—how they met, courtship, and so on. Was the baby conceived with both parents wishing for a child? How old were the parents at that point?

2. The physical and emotional state of mother during pregnancy:

   Was the pregnancy period complicated by illness, physical abuse, or substance abuse in one or both parents? Complications during delivery?

3. After the birth:

   Was the baby breast- or bottle-fed? Any complications regarding the baby's eating or sleeping habits? Was the baby often ill? If so, what were the causes?

4. Early childhood:

   When were the developmental milestones reached and how well were they negotiated—weaning from the bottle or breast, transition to solid foods, first steps, first words, toilet training? When did first separations take place (e.g., illness or withdrawal of a parent or other close family member, illness or hospitalization for the child)? Were there any traumatic events at that time to either child or family? When were siblings born, and how did the child react? When did day care or nursery school begin? How did the child and parent react to this? (Note: Preschool and school often herald the beginning of behavior difficulties, either in actuality or because they are noted by school staff.)

5. School years:

   How did the child adapt to school? Did the child make friends, visit with friends, have sleepovers, and so on? How did the child function academically? (School reports should be obtained.) Did the child have planned after-school activities? Were these supervised? Any hobbies? (In asking parents and their adolescent about the latter's developmental history, social workers must remember that many inner-city children are kept in constant activities outside of school because of the dangers in the neighborhood. This is, in fact, typical of city children in general. Children in urban settings cannot "go out and play" as routinely and as safely as suburban and rural children. It has been noted that, as a result, city children seem to grow up faster. Rural children tend to play at childhood games much longer than their city peers.)

The therapist needs to be flexible and sensitive to the parents while exploring their child's developmental history. If parents become distressed, it is more important to attend to their needs than to continue taking a history.

The developmental history and the questions the therapist asks can often be enlightening to parents. In hearing about the important normal components of a child's life (e.g., friends, sleepovers, activities), parents who are, for example, overly protective might begin to think about the social life of their child. Parents who have been severely deprived in their own childhood can begin to think about what their child may need that they have never thought of or experienced.

REFERRAL FOR PSYCHOLOGICAL TESTING

Psychological testing is rarely done on a routine basis. Typically, the therapist in a child guidance clinic can consult with the evaluating psychologist to see if testing is warranted (Mishne, 1983).

Psychological testing is often used to explore the nature of a child's problems in academic functioning. Specific types of learning disabilities or organic impairments can be diagnosed with more accuracy if standardized tests are used. Diagnostic issues can also be clarified and symptoms differentiated as to the nature of their source (i.e., developmental, psychodynamic, or neurological).

Standardized tests include the Rorschach, the Thematic Apperception Test (TAT), and the Wechsler Intelligence Scale for Children (WISC). The Rorschach and the TAT are referred to as projective tests: children are asked to associate to the deliberately enigmatic pictures and describe what they think is happening in the pictures. Children will usually associate to themes common to their own lives. For example, a child living in chaotic, violent circumstances might impose these perceptions fairly consistently in association to the pictures of the projective tests.

The WISC and the Stanford-Binet tests evaluate IQ and cognitive functioning. The subtests of these evaluate specific aspects of intellectual functioning in verbal, nonverbal, and performance areas.

If psychological testing is used, the evaluating psychologist must be fluent in the language of the child being evaluated, as well as familiar with geographical linguistic idiosyncrasies. (For example, West Indian children who say "sweets" instead of "candy" reflect the dialect of their community.) Therapists should review their client's test results with the examiner to understand the findings. This will aid them in reporting the results sensitively and intelligently to the parents and child.

CHAPTER 5

THE INITIAL SESSION

CASE EXAMPLE: MICKEY, A CHILD WITH AN EATING DISORDER

Therapist's Report

Mickey was a slight, thin six-year-old whose head was somewhat large for his body. For his first therapy session, he separated easily from his parents, who went into the waiting area.

Mickey was quite engaging and smiled through almost the entire session. He appeared to settle down immediately, and he confided his worries to his new therapist. He described how he was afraid of certain things: new foods, leaving his parents, and clowns ("because of their faces"). The therapist asked what frightened him about a clown's face, but Mickey couldn't describe this fear further. The therapist mentioned that she had heard that he also feared birthday parties even if clowns weren't there. Mickey said that was so and added that he also feared his own birthday party but didn't know why. He described not liking to draw and didn't want to draw a picture (and, in fact, did not draw one for his therapist). He told the therapist details about the foods he liked: fried chicken nuggets from only a certain fast food store, dried cereal, and Oreo cookies.

In response to a question about the saddest day of his life, Mickey described how his best friend, Sara, moved away with her family. He admitted planning to marry Sara and told the social worker how he had formed a detective club with her. They reportedly had "long talks" together on the phone. Mickey described another "bad" experience: recently he and two friends were chased out of a school bathroom by some "bigger boys." Mickey was terrified of using the bathroom after this and stated, "God knows what would have happened if they caught us." His eyes were enormous as he said this.

Mickey talked of not being able to draw or write well and admitted having problems tying his shoelaces even though he knew he was "an excellent student." He said that the best day of his life was when he was playing softball and made a spectacular catch; he demonstrated this for his therapist. He slowly inscribed an arc in the air with his hand, demonstrating how he caught the ball as it came close to the ground. He was disappointed that his parents had not seen this, nor was there a photograph of this to show.

Mickey's three wishes were these:

1. He would have a Rose rookie baseball card (i.e., a card depicting Pete Rose as a rookie). Mickey said that this card was worth hundreds of dollars and that his father wanted this card, too.
2. His mommy would like baseball cards.
3. He would meet "every baseball player in the world who is alive."

Mickey reported loving baseball, collecting baseball cards with his father, watching movies about science fiction and "heroes," and reading mysteries.

In response to a question about nightmares, Mickey described a puzzling dream. He said that he dreamed that he "ate a book." The therapist said that she had heard that he was very smart and read a great deal. How was this a nightmare? Mickey replied, "That's what I don't know."

Mickey occasionally made reference in this session to "telling the lady" (the evaluating psychiatrist) various aspects of his narrative.

The therapist asked if he was disappointed not to be seeing "the lady" anymore. Mickey said no, he liked it here and was willing to come again.

During the session, the therapist noted that while Mickey smiled a great deal, he rarely made eye contact.

The family seemed to take a long time to leave the clinic after Mickey's initial session. The therapist passed them in the lobby a half hour after the session had ended and overheard Mickey elaborating to his parents on what he told his "new lady."

Evaluation and Psychodynamic Formulation

Mickey was seen as a bright, appealing, highly verbal child who presented long-standing difficulties with anxiety and obsessional thinking that manifested themselves in many areas of his life, including sleeping, eating, and bowel functioning. He had a history of separation anxiety and phobic avoidance. Despite this, he functioned well socially and intellectually.

The content of Mickey's first session was typical of his later ones. Mickey had easy access to fears of death, and there was an occasional blurring of his ego boundaries. He clearly was concerned about his parents' marriage and tried to diminish their anger at each other.

The history of emotional difficulties of Mickey's parents led the therapist to hypothesize that Mickey's separation anxiety was in part a form of guilt over separating from his two very fragile parents.

Diagnosis

Given the severity of his anxiety and the weakness of his ego functioning, Mickey was diagnosed as a borderline child. Borderline children typically have a multiplicity of symptoms. Although they tend to maintain their capacity for reality testing, in spite of thought disorders such as hallucinations and bizarre delusions, they do display a chronic, free-floating, excessive anxiety that makes them fearful of the world and of separating from their caregivers. The high degree of phobic content and its many variations and the chronic free-floating anxiety and ego weakness depicted in Mickey's symptom history often lead to a prognosis of borderline personality disorder in adulthood.

THE DIAGNOSTIC ASSESSMENT

Presenting Problem

Mickey R., age six, was referred to our clinic by a private psychiatrist who saw him for initial evaluation for the possibility of treating him in an analysis. Mickey suffered from many phobias, fetishes, and rituals. His symptoms included a fear of attending birthday parties, including his own; fears about using the toilet, both at home and in school; fears of clowns and of masks; great anxiety on separation from parents and home; bowel retention to the point of great physical discomfort; food fetishes (eating only two or three kinds of food, prepared in particular ways); reading several newspapers daily in a specific order; and, finally, an excessive preoccupation with death and disaster (which he read about in the newspaper and saw on television). Additionally, it emerged in the intake session that Mickey's parents had marital difficulties. Mr. and Mrs. R. argued over discipline and the upbringing of the child, over money, and over Mr. R.'s inconsistent employment history.

Because it was felt that Mickey's parents could not afford a private fee and that a traditional analysis of several times a week might not be appropriate for a child with such a fragile psychic structure, referral was made to our clinic. (Mickey was seen once a week, his parents were seen once a week, and there were occasional family therapy sessions. These ceased after Mickey complained that the family sessions were too upsetting; he preferred individual sessions with his therapist.)

Mickey's Family History

Mr. and Mrs. R. were an intelligent, articulate couple who lived with their children, Mickey, age six, and Nancy, age two, in a modest apartment. Mr. and Mrs. R., a Jewish working-class couple, each with some college education, were both overweight and somewhat babyish in appearance and manner. Both were functioning in work situations beneath their capacities: Mrs. R. was a bank teller, and Mr. R. was sporadically employed at flea markets selling baseball cards, comics, and so on.

Mr. and Mrs. R. had been married for twelve years. The first four years of their marriage were described by both as a very happy and financially secure time; Mr. R. was then contentedly employed in a Wall Street corporation, and Mrs. R. was a computer programmer. Mickey, a planned baby, arrived after four years of marriage. During his wife's pregnancy, Mr. R. began to experience job difficulties and was let go, reportedly due to the changing economic climate. As he had only two years of college, he found it difficult to gain similar employment and finally began his own business, a candy store on the East Side. Due to the high rent, this business only broke even. The marriage became increasingly problematic, as Mickey had many eating difficulties in infancy and Mrs. R. had "great separation anxieties" regarding him. Mr. R. also became very bound up with Mickey, to the exclusion of his wife.

Nancy, twenty-one months, was an unplanned baby. It is of note that she was developing normally and was experiencing none of her brother's early difficulties.

An additional strain on the marriage had been Mr. R.'s compulsive gambling (poker playing). Both Mr. and Mrs. R. insisted that he always won (and in fact he won in the range of five hundred dollars per game). Another considerable strain was the overinvolvement of both sets of grandparents. Mr. R.'s parents, in particular, were described as highly intrusive people, and Mr. R. admitted always feeling angry and embarrassed by them. Mrs. R. was angered by their preferential treatment of Nancy over Mickey. Mickey verbalized his dislike for them.

Mickey was a friendly, likable, intellectually gifted child who reported functioning well in school but was fearful of any new experiences. He was surprisingly high functioning given his multiple phobias. He was especially afraid of death and of physical attack from the outside world. However, he had many friends and made a quick friendship with his social worker, whom he referred to as "my little lady" (he called his previous psychiatrist "my lady").

Mickey's problems included fears of clowns and masks, food fetishes, constipation related to poor eating habits, fear of using the school bathroom, and fears about death and violence. He also had certain rituals, primarily around reading newspapers in a certain order; he read three newspapers daily in the same order: headlines, movie reviews, sports reviews.

Mickey had psychological testing, and his IQ was found to be in the superior range with special abilities in verbal and mathematical tasks. He did show a possibility of "soft signs," as evidenced by his poor coordination (he had difficulty buttoning his shirts properly, put clothing on inside out, etc.), which he was very sensitive about.

Mickey was an excellent student and attended a class for the intellectually gifted. He had many friends, mainly from school, and was a very engaging, personable, sociable child. It is of note that in therapy sessions he was almost always smiling, showing a full set of teeth. This appeared to be related to anxiety (however, his mother was almost always smiling as well). Mickey often smiled in situations where affect and verbal dialogue did not match. It is possible that his smile was related to oral aggression, given his difficulties with his aggressive drives (especially given his multiple phobias).

Significant Events

Mickey entered a play group at eighteen months but had to leave because he was, according to his mother, "afraid of one child in particular for no real reasons." He always had trouble separating, and Mrs. R. never felt safe leaving him. At three and a half, he began nursery school and "screamed" at first.

Mickey developed ear infections at age three, and according to his parents, his fears began after this. The year before starting therapy, Mickey and two friends were chased out of the school bathroom by bigger boys. Mickey was terrified of using the school bathroom after this and stated to his social worker, "God knows what would have happened."

In addition, Mickey had always been a poor sleeper and a poor eater, had been chronically constipated, bit his nails, and picked at his lips. He was markedly nonaggressive with other children, including his adolescent baby-sitter, and was preoccupied with death.

History of Presenting Problem

Mrs. R. described Mickey as "never easy to leave." Mr. R. said that his wife would never leave the boy with a sitter, other than the grandparents, and she confirmed this, saying that she always worried about him, from infancy on. This was in marked contrast to her feelings about Nancy, whom she described as "much easier."

At eighteen months Mickey was afraid of the other children in his play group who were more aggressive. When he started nursery school, his mother had to stay with him for a month, and she described this as a "disaster." During the summer that he was three and a half years old, his parents were having a "crisis" in their marriage, with Mr. R. often angry and Mrs. R. often crying. Although Mrs. R. thought that Mickey was upset by this, he was fine in the beginning of his second year of nursery school. However, he then became afraid of a dance teacher who came once a week and would cry hysterically on that day when his mother left him at school. He "worked it out," and the next year, when this same woman became his regular teacher, there was no problem.

For his first month of first grade, in a new school, Mickey again cried when his mother left, but then was all right. When he started therapy, he reportedly loved school but was afraid to go to an after-school sports program, although he'd planned to go with his best friend.

Mrs. R. reported that her son was usually easy to take places (outings, museums, etc.) but that it was hard to get him to leave the house. She said that on a recent weekend trip he complained the whole time and wanted to go home.

Developmental History

Mickey was a planned child. His mother was "a little disappointed" that he wasn't a girl, but he was "a nice child." She breast-fed him for five months ("He was up all the time, so I was nursing all the time"). During Mickey's infancy the family was going through a hard time, because Mr. R. was anticipating losing his job. Mrs. R. enjoyed nursing and felt "tranquil" while she nursed, but she described it as "hard." She was "very nervous" with the baby, and his father bathed him. The paternal grandparents came once a week and were helpful.

At two months, when solid foods were introduced, Mickey began to sleep for three or four hours at a time. Mrs. R.'s anxiety lessened as she began to get more sleep, and the second six months of Mickey's first year were "nice."

At eleven months Mickey's eating diminished, both in variety and quantity. At thirteen months he became ill with a virus, and afterward he continued to refuse to eat. He also had some persistent diarrhea. The pediatrician wasn't concerned, but Mrs. R. became frantic and did "crazy things." Eventually, Mickey began to lose weight. He didn't resume eating solids for several months and according to Mrs. R., drank only sugar water from a bottle and ate only Rice Krispies. At age six, he was still a picky eater, eating only one food at a time. Mickey reported that he "can't sit at the table" with others, doesn't enjoy eating, and eats only cheese sandwiches and cold cereal.

Mickey gave up his daytime bottle at two years and gave up thumb sucking when the dentist told him to, but replaced it with nail biting.

Mickey had always been prone to diarrhea and constipation, for which bran was prescribed. When he entered therapy, he was still suffering from constipation. At the time of the consultation, Mrs. R. was trying to discontinue giving him mineral oil and an emulsifier.

Toilet training was accomplished at around age three. Mickey was trained for urine first, and with no particular difficulty. Bowel training was "rough," according to Mrs. R., although she didn't remember it well. She did recall that at one point he had a bowel accident after school ("He'd been holding back"). Again, bran was prescribed, which helped. Mrs. R. reported that Mickey had refused to wipe himself until the previous year. She claimed that when Mickey was constipated, his whole personality changed. He became more lethargic, spent much time sitting on the toilet, and "worried a lot." Mrs. R. admitted that she had always had mild constipation herself, a fact she disclosed to Mickey.

Mickey never slept well and did not sleep through the night until he was four years old. After the family moved (when Mickey was two), one parent had to stay with him until he fell asleep. This continued past nursery school. Mrs. R. admitted that she was the same way as a child.

At about twenty-two months, while his grandmother was babysitting one evening, Mickey seemed to become terrified of his crib and switched abruptly to sleeping in a bed. Mrs. R. reported that he still awakened at night but that he didn't wake his parents.

Mickey's physical development was described as somewhat slow. He sat at nine months and began to crawl at the same time, but "dragged his body." (Mr. R. was said to have had poor coordination and to have been misdiagnosed as having muscular dystrophy as a child.) Mickey had somewhat poor coordination and had trouble with skipping, climbing, and running. His handwriting was poor, although he had been working on it and it was improving.

Mickey had always had a long attention span. His mother reported that when he was an infant, he would look at a mobile for hours and that he could always entertain himself. She said that she had always enjoyed playing with him and that she was sometimes in awe of his mind. She revealed that his teacher thought he was "a genius" and said that he enjoyed reading and was currently fascinated by mysteries.

Mrs. R. reported that Mickey used to masturbate "a lot." He would go into his room, get undressed, and wrap himself up. He became upset if anyone came in without knocking. He expressed worry that his penis was too small, and he didn't want anybody to see it. He told his mother that he knew about babies "from Mr. Rogers" and never asked her how they were made. When his sister was born, he asked why she didn't have a penis, and Mrs. R. thought he was worried that he might lose his.

Nancy was born when Mickey was three. The pregnancy was unplanned, and both parents were upset, primarily because of money problems. Mr. R. was struggling to maintain a small retail business at the time. His parents told Mickey early about the pregnancy, and he seemed happy. His friends had siblings, and he said he wanted a brother or sister because when he grew up and people died, he'd have no one. Mrs. R. reported that the baby was "easy" and that Mickey didn't seem upset by her arrival but that his nail biting increased after she was born.

Current Description

Mrs. R. described her son as bright, aware, warm, and kind, but she also reported that he was "compulsive" and would play many games of Monopoly or Scrabble in a row, unable to stop ("He can't shut off") and that he sometimes couldn't stop talking and talked so incessantly that his father sometimes screamed, "Stop!" She said that he continued talking even if the other person left the room.

Mrs. R. said that Mickey had always had trouble with changes in routine and that he got upset when he had to change from one season's clothing to the next.

The year prior to treatment, Mrs. R. said, Mickey was preoccupied with death and dying and had asked his grandparents when they were going to die (a friend's father had died a few years earlier).

Mrs. R. reported that Mickey was interested in baseball, although he didn't play well, and in mysteries (he and a friend had a "club" that seemed to center around writing mystery stories) and that he read very well and liked to read the Arts and Leisure section of the newspaper to see what would be on TV.

To other children, Mickey seemed to have a helpless quality that elicited concern. At school, for example, other children retrieved his outer clothing for him and zipped his jacket. He was unable to tie his shoes. He was not overtly aggressive and removed himself from potential fights. On one occasion, Mrs. R. said, a child pushed him and he became "hysterical." Mrs. R. described her son as a "self-punisher": if, for instance, she threatened to take away his baseball cards, he would rip them up himself.

Mickey was reportedly messy and unwilling to help at home, which bothered his mother. However, his father was described as being the same way.

This diagnostic assessment was written in a format that is typical of those used in most child guidance agencies. In the past, many child therapists utilized the Metapsychological Profile developed by Anna Freud. Although that was an excellent diagnostic tool, it is rarely used in most agencies today and is more reflective of classical psychoanalytic thinking.

CASE EXAMPLE: MAIA, AN ADOLESCENT WITH MULTICULTURAL ISSUES

Maia was the eldest child of immigrant Asian parents. She had two younger brothers ages ten and four. Maia came to treatment at the age of fourteen. She was referred to the clinic by her school guidance counselor (a friend of the social worker-therapist), who suggested that she request the social worker. When Maia came to the clinic office, she told the receptionist that she had an appointment with the therapist (although she did not). She later admitted to making this up since she was determined to have the social worker as her therapist. Maia described the following history:

The precipitating problem was that Maia's mother had made a very serious and dramatic suicide attempt by jumping into a river. (This was the most recent of many suicide attempts on her mother's part; in fact, it emerged much later in treatment that Maia's mother's family had had at least one other suicide and that Maia's father had also made one serious attempt at suicide in his early twenties.) Her mother had been hospitalized at a city hospital, despite her husband's objections. Maia, as the eldest child and only daughter, was desperately frightened and depressed, and she was frantic to try to help her mother.

Maia gave an impressive family history: Mr. and Mrs. Ling had married in their early twenties in their Asian country of origin and had then emigrated to the United States. Mrs. Ling came from a family of high nobility in her country (her mother had been the first woman doctor in the country's capital). Her family opposed her marriage, feeling that Mr. Ling was neither good enough for her nor from as high-powered a family. Mr. Ling had been an officer in the army (which was notable for its corruption), had been caught in some misconduct (exactly what this was never became clear to the therapist), and had then attempted suicide to "save face." The Lings lived in this country on income from investments in the stock market. As the market began to drop, Mr. Ling began to blame his wife for withholding family funds (which actually weren't hers). This resulted in long and tedious harangues, culminating in physical violence between the parents. At night the Ling children were subjected to these scenes, which kept them up until the early hours of the morning. Mrs. Ling received periodic injuries that necessitated medical treatment.

Mrs. Ling received a master's degree in early childhood education from an Ivy League university in this country. Her husband was instrumental in encouraging her to do this, although her investment in this career was unclear. She was unable to hold a job for long as a teacher and soon became pregnant with her first child, Maia. Two boys were born, four and ten years later. Maia, as eldest and as daughter, was culturally expected to be second mother to her brothers and frequently denied herself things that they, as boys, were entitled to.

The social worker noted Maia's despair and depressed affect. Her grades suffered badly. Although she attended a school for intellectually gifted children, she was in danger of failing out of school. Her family took great pride in her intellectual achievements. The Lings had considered moving to California but, based on Maia's acceptance to a prestigious school, decided to remain in New York.

In her first session, Maia told the therapist something about the cultural values of her family. One tradition in this particular Asian culture (where the role of hierarchy and idealization of authority are very powerful) was to assign familial titles to significant adults outside the family structure, thus conferring upon them nearly familial stature in the hierarchy. For example, the family's sponsor to this country (a social worker) was given the title of "grandmother," a great honor. When her therapist asked Maia, "What would I be called?" she immediately responded (having obviously already thought about this) that "aunt" seemed to fit. Maia said that she would like to continue therapy and that she could bring her mother to her next session to meet the social worker.

ASSESSMENT AND HISTORY

Shortly after Maia's second session, one of her younger brothers attempted to accompany her to two or three sessions. He was an aggressive boy, as described by his sister, who was used to getting his way, often at her expense. He was concerned that his sister was pulling away from the family; he threatened to follow her everywhere to make her feel guilty. The social worker made the decision to protect the privacy of Maia's sessions but offered the boy family therapy via the hospital or individual therapy. He refused both but was able to leave Maia to her own sessions. Although the family had two conjoint therapists at the hospital, all members (except Mr. Ling) often requested meetings with the social worker.

Maia described violent arguments between her mother and father. (These began around 11 P.M. and continued until 2 or 3 A.M.). In order to deal with this, the worker taught Maia to call the police; their arrival ended the fights for the time being, although Mrs. Ling couldn't bring herself to press charges. At this point, the treatment team had involved every protective agency in the city in this case, but little could be done as the children were not physically abused.

The family income from the stock market continued to severely decline, and Mr. Ling would go daily to the stock exchange to study the figures. The treatment team had great concerns over the family's low income: they learned that Mr. Ling was violently opposed to welfare and that he had threatened to sell his wife and daughter into prostitution first or to have the family make a mass suicide pact. Mr. Ling called himself a "samurai in spirit, a Confucian in practice." He also greatly admired Nazi Germany. When the worker questioned Maia about the suicide pact, she laughed and said, "Of course I wouldn't agree to that." Moreover, she was able to outline the various steps she could take, if necessary: call the therapist, call police, call neighbors, go to a friend's house. (She frequently employed all of the above.) The social worker felt that Maia was a bright, articulate adolescent who was depressed and overwhelmed and terrified by the chaos of her family and the enormity of their difficulties. Maia appeared eager for help and seemed to make very good use of counseling. She clearly needed help in dealing with her family's problems; in addition, she needed to be restored to her own life as an adolescent. Individual treatment was recommended, with family treatment implemented as soon as possible, if her parents were willing to attend.

CASE EXAMPLE: A FORENSIC INTERVIEW AND ASSESSMENT WITH AN OLDER ADOLESCENT

Jack was an eighteen-year-old referred to the clinic by the court system. The court requested specifically an evaluation of his potential for future violence.

Jack lived in a small town. He was arrested for firing his gun out the window of his parents' suburban house. Several bullets entered a neighbor's house through the window; fortunately, no one was at home at that juncture. Jack denied any hostile motive in firing out the window. He said that it was stupid on his part to have done so, that he just wasn't thinking. He claimed to be shooting at pigeons, which he described as "a nuisance."

Jack's social worker at the clinic had to point out to him that he would have to report his findings to the court, as this was an evaluation and not treatment. Jack made a poor impression upon his social worker. He spoke in monosyllables and appeared expressionless; he had a very guarded style in general.

His social worker elicited the following factual material from Jack: He lived at home with his parents. By day he worked for his father's construction firm. In the evening he worked as a projectionist for a pornographic movie theater.

When asked if he had friends, Jack shrugged and said yes, but he could not describe a single friendship. He said that occasionally he picked up girls in a local bar; his approach was to ask them explicitly and crudely if they wanted to have sex. Occasionally he went hunting with his male relatives. When asked, Jack claimed that nothing was on his mind when he shot at birds. He denied any angry thoughts at anyone and said that he simply had an impulse to shoot at birds. He felt he had no need of therapy and had come only because his lawyer urged him to cooperate with the court.

Jack's social worker was in a quandary. After two more sessions he grew to have some empathy for Jack and felt bad about having to report to the court. At the same time, Jack's lack of relatedness was increasingly frustrating to him.

Analysis

Jack's social worker understandably felt frustration and also pity for his client. He needed to be reminded that his work with this client was only a prognostic evaluation and not treatment.

What was important in this evaluation was that Jack appeared to have no value for human life. Even as a hunter, he behaved irresponsibly (by firing his rifle in a suburban neighborhood). His lack of relationships and general unresponsiveness were also a cause for concern.

It was felt that Jack should, at a minimum, receive ongoing supervision from the court; treatment was recommended, if he was willing to participate seriously. Further evaluation, with psychological testing and a psychiatric interview, was also recommended.

CHAPTER 6

PLAY THERAPY

THE MATERIALS OF PLAY THERAPY

Child therapists use play techniques with children. Play is an important means of allowing children to express their real or fantasized preoccupations. Anna Freud (1951) believed that the therapist could know and understand the child's responses, attitudes, and impulses by witnessing the child's play. Play is a form of free association for children in response to events in their everyday life.

The materials of play therapy need not be elaborate but should be inviting to the child. This feature assists in helping the work of play therapy to begin.

Child therapists often equip their offices in unique ways. Often, therapists will include toys or books that are idiosyncratic to their own tastes and that reflect something of the therapist's sensibilities and subjectivity.

In actuality, there need not be a great array of toys. What is important is that whatever equipment or crafts are employed be in good condition and be safe to use. When toys and games are broken or too old, children experience this as a communication that they (as clients) are not valued or important enough to be regarded with consideration. The children and adolescents that social workers meet with have already experienced serious emotional and material deprivation. I believe that it is important to have an office that is cheerful, pleasant, and welcoming, with play materials that might excite and expand the creative potential in each child. The setting of play therapy can communicate something important. Hopes for a decent future—both in terms of the child's home life and in terms of fulfillment of the child's potential—are sometimes inspired by the therapist's office itself, as revealed in children's dialogues with their therapist about how they would like to live someday.

In my office I like to have new crayons or colored markers that are washable and nontoxic. Paper can be white or colored (children's use of dark or colored paper often reflects affects like depression and anger). Clay that is naturally soft is preferable to work with; it is easy to manipulate and can be bought (e.g., Play-Doh) or made at home. Puppets that are hand or finger puppets are easy to manipulate; these should include both animals that are friendly and those that are ferocious in appearance.

Games might include such perennial favorites as checkers, Chinese checkers, and dominoes. A deck of playing cards is useful with older children and adolescents who don't like to speak.

Bags of inexpensive soldiers are helpful. If possible, it is useful to have some toys that are currently popular—especially action figures, half-human–half-beast dolls, and superheroes and heroines. Therapists can ask children if they have any favorite toy that they would like the therapist to get. If a child already owns this, I like to suggest that the child bring it in to show me.

Doll figures should be reflective of race and ethnicity. Dolls like Barbie or Ken should reflect the race of the child, as these often can represent the young client's ego ideals and fantasies about life in the future as an adult. Children need to be able to see their race and ethnicity in a positive light. Small dolls that reflect a family are also helpful in playing out family dramas and should be in multicultural sets.

I like to have books of children's fairy tales that have beautiful illustrations. Children can free-associate to these easily, and the illustrations can elicit further fantasy. Fairy tales are often metaphors for the struggles and issues of childhood.

Some games don't require very much beyond pencil and paper. Hangman, other word games, connect-the-dots—all these can be helpful as jumping-off points both for interaction with the therapist and for free association into unconscious content.

I suggest using soft sponge balls to play with; the office should contain no toy that can be used as an actual weapon. I also suggest not using paints or water or clay that can be thrown. The office should not be so fancy that children can't feel free, but some materials invite aggression from children, especially if the materials can be thrown!

Some children love to make crafts. This is a lovely way for a therapist and child to work cooperatively on a project (a metaphor for the relationship that will evolve). Crafts should not be overly complex or frustrating and must match the child's capabilities. It is advisable to allow children to bring the finished craft project home. The project is often emblematic of a tie to the therapist and the therapy itself, which is a process that is conducted as a joint venture.

When working in an inpatient setting, such as a residential treatment center or a school, the therapist needs to be aware that the children are often highly competitive with each other and will often boast about what they made or did in therapy. In one such setting, a therapist learned that the boys she worked with envied the girls who were constructing pompoms and wanted to learn to make them too. Although crafts take on an individual meaning with each child, inpatient children often copy each other's special games. For example, one child liked to play that she was injured and required an arm cast, which reflected her own sense of psychological damage. This inspired other children in the school to play the same game. This therapist realized that she had to limit the game to the office; it was becoming problematic in the school setting to have so many children walking around displaying fictitious bodily injuries!

In working with children who have been sexually abused, it is important to have a set of anatomically correct dolls. With trauma as extreme as sexual abuse, it is easier for the child to demonstrate what happened by utilizing the dolls than to describe the experience in words. I would note that these dolls are often unattractive to look at; in my experience, they are usually only compelling to the child if abuse has actually occurred.

In group therapy with children, a therapist might consider having several group games so that the children can break into subgroups if they wish. The subgroups of one latency age group united only once—in their last session. The children found a skein of twine and tied it to various pieces of furniture in the room. The therapist, realizing that the group wished to stay tied together, had to intervene to keep the children from leaving the room and venturing into the corridors of the community center. They expressed a wish to tie up other aspects of the center to keep anyone from leaving. Clearly, the therapist then had to reflect upon the sadness of terminating with this group.

THE USE OF METAPHOR IN PLAY THERAPY

The distinguishing difference between child and adult therapy is that the child therapist must learn to understand the complex metaphors of play and fantasy to an even greater degree than those who treat only adults. This task is daunting initially; it can seem like the task of a professional translator who must translate relentlessly. The therapist and client must create a mutually understandable meaning. Sometimes, the context of a therapy session with a child is so obscure that it must be witnessed over several sessions to become clear.

It is useful to witness the game or action being played in a child's therapy session and to attempt to describe this to oneself in a variety of ways. For example, in the session mentioned above of a group terminating treatment, the therapist first observed to herself that everyone was tying everything up. She wondered why. Then she understood this in the context of the group's impending dissolution: she reflected that if everyone stayed tied to everything and to each other, then they could never leave. By then, the group could vehemently second her interpretation and begin to talk again.

When struggling with the meaning of a child's fantasy or play, the therapist needs to consider the child's developmental stage and difficulties, what is currently happening in the child's everyday life and family life, and what is happening between the child and therapist. It is clear than an interpretation of a child's play reflects the child's many levels of functioning. The internal workings of the psyche, developmental milestones, interpersonal psychodynamics, and familial and school systemic issues—these are all opportunities for enactment in the child's play.

Issues of separation and differentiation are probably the most stressful tasks for human beings to resolve. They are possibly the most common source of anxiety for children, whether the focus is autonomous striving or actual loss of a loved one.

THEORIES OF PLAY

Play can represent a multitude of tasks that can generate not only anxiety but also pleasure. Play that is repetitive in therapy is a way of expressing a conflict by way of repetition compulsion, or it can be a way of repeating a problem or dilemma that needs resolution and mastery. Children can repeat an act over and over to highlight the importance of its meaning or to figure out different ways of solving a problem, which is symbolically posed and enacted in play, that is a source of conflict for them.

In the chapter on posttraumatic stress, a description is given of a child who enacts over and over to his therapist a murder scene he has witnessed. Witnessing a murder would be a source of enormous stress and anxiety for anyone. This child is compelled to repeat this game to commemorate the event and to communicate its importance to his therapist. With her help, he tries to find relief from the terror that this memory has imposed. His acting out behavior can be related to this as well. He has been overstimulated and enacts his perpetual conflict in all of his interpersonal relationships. The traumatic memory acts as a trigger to his sense of perpetual danger and his need to be continually on the offensive in interpersonal relationships.

Play can also be repetitive as an effort to resolve a dilemma. For example, playing house is a game that children frequently play to enact their fantasies about the future as an adult. The fantasies can supply inventive possible solutions to the developmental demands of the future. In Chapter 16 a girls' group plays out a family drama: an adolescent girl going out on her first date. Some of the girls in the group love this game and want to play the adolescent girl. Other (younger) girls admit hating this and want to play the safer part of the grandmother or aunt or mother, that is, a woman who helps out family members or sets limits on them. This play demonstrates many levels of anxiety about the future, but it also expresses and anticipates the delights of love, sexuality, and freedom that adulthood can bring. The very same subject that is a source of anxiety can also be a subject and source of pleasure. The different forms that repetition takes in their play can enable children to develop new strategies for future use.

Altman (in Skolnick and Warshaw, 1992) has remarked that the child's natural propensity to play allows the therapist to participate as both an old and a new object. A variety of roles, both internal and interpersonal, can be played in different interactions; these aid in gaining insight into past history within the experiences of the current therapeutic relationship. In the relational context, the therapist is both old and new. For example, a child who plays out being abused can also play out the protective function of the therapist. That is, the child might play the role of victim or might identify totally with the therapist as protector (e.g., by playing that they are on the same team).

INTERPRETATION

All play needn't be interpreted in therapy. Some children even request that the therapist remain silent at times. If that is the case, I suggest respecting this if at all possible. I do not believe that the therapist as a blank screen is useful with children. This style of work is safe, perhaps, in that there is no risk of being incorrect. In a relational style of therapeutic work, it is a given that the treatment process is active and is a process of continual self-regulating and influencing the feeling states of others. The individual's sense of self is continually regulated by feelings and thoughts and also by interaction with others. The best therapeutic relationships model new ways of thinking and interacting and can be a reeducation for clients about the possibilities of living.

Case Example: Interpretations in Mid Phase of Treatment

Rolando, age eight, resided in residential treatment. His sister, Olivia, age ten, was fortunate to have been adopted. Her parents were without children and were a fine family. Rolando harbored a wish to eventually go to live in their home, although Olivia's parents were firm in their decision not to allow this. They nonetheless permitted Rolando to visit his sister frequently.

When Olivia's adoptive mother became pregnant, Rolando played out the following game in treatment. He took the dollhouse and moved one child-doll from room to room, having the doll look for a place to sleep.

The therapist commented sympathetically that this was, in a way, Rolando's situation too; now that Olivia's parents were having a baby, it might feel as if there was no room for him there—that this was hard. After allowing Rolando to express his sadness and anger at the family in the following sessions, the therapist told him that she would try hard to find him a family of his own.

Children who have experienced continual impulsive, brutal, and abusive behavior can learn from therapy that there are other ways of being involved with people and other ways of thinking about themselves. This can happen if the child therapist is willing to play many parts. Sometimes the therapist is an educator, sometimes a helper, sometimes a screen for projections of the most negative nature, and sometimes an idealized self-object. If the therapist can accept the child's most malignant feelings about others and the world, then the real therapeutic work can begin: teaching the child something important about him/herself.

Case Example: The Negative Therapeutic Reaction in Play Therapy

The negative therapeutic reaction is a term that describes the type of client that needs to actively destroy and reject any help that they might receive from treatment. Seinfeld (1990) has described the negative therapeutic situation in child treatment. Children and adolescents who are extremely aggressive, undersocialized and antisocial often reject help and sympathy. Children of this type experience potentially helpful others as obstacles or as engulfing, as attacking their sense of omnipotence.

These children have experienced abuse and excessive harsh criticism from potential caregivers. The children have learned to be wary of interaction with any potential authority figure. The following case vignette illustrates the negative therapeutic reaction in play therapy.

Dina, a compulsively aggressive ten-year-old girl, was abusive to other children and staff members. She often bullied smaller children and attempted to physically push her therapist and other staff around. She had been subjected to physical and sexual abuse at home. After many physical encounters with Dina, her therapist became considerably angry and frustrated in her work. She decided to confront Dina. After being pushed physically, she loudly responded, "Why should I put up with this? I don't have to put up with this." Dina looked startled and said, "You have to; you're my therapist." The therapist replied, "No, I don't have to, not when you are being abusive to me." She went on to say that Dina could use any language to her to describe her feelings, that she could in fact say anything she wanted and she would listen, but that she would not allow herself to be abused.

Dina's therapist also explained in that session, and in many others, that she wanted her client to learn to protect herself, because she had been so unfairly treated in the abuse she had experienced. She said that she wanted Dina to learn to use words to describe her feelings and to fight with. She made it clear that she would continue to work with Dina but that if the physical abuse resumed, she would end the session. Dina was visibly impressed by this intervention and said that she wanted to learn more about how to use words to fight.

Analysis

In this vignette there is no real interpretation; rather, behavior was modeled for the child about what is acceptable in everyday life. In later sessions, the therapist can help Dina explore her reactions to her early experiences of abuse and understand how she learned to structure and organize her life around her constant expectation of maltreatment, namely, by becoming the aggressor before bad things could happen to her.

INTERPRETATION OF PLAY, PLAYING, AND THE USE OF THE THERAPIST AS OBJECT

The question of when to interpret play content is difficult to assess. Winnicott discussed the problem of premature interpretation and how this can shut down dialogue. Fairbairn thought that premature interpretation could drive a symptom into further repression. Winnicott (1958) once commented that "what matters to the patient is not so much the interpretation as the willingness to help." Winnicott (1955) also thought that even mistakes or failures on the part of the analyst were made use of by the patient.

Winnicott offered a rule of thumb for interpreting the meaning of unconscious phenomena in his concept of "the well-timed interpretation." He suggested that an interpretation is accurate when (1) the therapist knows the patient so well that she can fairly well predict the patient's response, (2) the patient responds with an affective response, (3) the patient can elaborate upon the interpretation with further associations or information, and (4) the patient can bring in unconscious or dream material in response to the interpretation.

In child treatment, clients only occasionally bring in dreams to discuss, but certainly the formula that Winnicott offered is an inspired one. Interpretation with children is best saved for the time when the therapist believes that such commentary on the deeper meaning or implications of a child's narrative can be heard and utilized by the child. This kind of commentary can be done in the form of play. According to Winnicott (1971) "psychotherapy takes place in the overlap of two areas of playing, that of the patient and that of the therapist. Psychotherapy has to do with two people playing together." Winnicott went on to suggest that, in a sense, the therapist is also used as an object of play. C. Bollas (1989) thought that therapists also use free association at times in creating an interpretation of meaning for their clients, thereby revealing their own reality. We saw in the examples in this chapter (and will see in clinical vignettes throughout this book) that children often use the therapist not only to play out projections but also to try out new ideas and new ways of relating. Hence, interpretations are, at best, ideas about being and meaning that the child and the therapist can formulate together in a mutual quest.

As the therapeutic relationship evolves, the child acquires a deeper understanding of the nature of psychotherapy. Here are two case examples of treatment in the middle phase of therapy.

Case Example

Jose, a nine-year-old, lived with his grandmother for the first three years of his life. His mother joined them after being released from prison for drug dealing. Mother and grandmother were locked in anger at each other, but they remained mutually dependent. (They usually kept their conversation to a minimum at home.) Despite their ongoing hostility, both women sincerely loved Jose.

Jose's therapist met with him in a school setting. She noted that he had begun to move into a much more related phase in his treatment. During one session, as he worked on a drawing, he began to sing an advertising jingle. When his therapist began to hum the jingle too, Jose laughed and said, "It went from my head to your head and back again." He continued, "I knew you would do that." His therapist commented that they seemed to know each other very well now and then asked him if he liked coming. Jose answered, "I don't like coming, I *love* coming." She replied that she loved seeing him, that they enjoyed their time together.

Case Example

In a session in the middle phase of his treatment, Mickey (previously described) drew a picture of a game. In the game he drew a round face attached by a string (like a Christmas ornament) and then he said to his therapist, "This is you, Winky the Adventurer." His therapist asked what Winky did. Mickey replied that Winky shot arrows out of his head that hit the targets. His therapist said (knowing him very well by this time), "Like the way I say things sometimes that make sense to you?" Mickey nodded.

In their play, both Jose and Mickey were demonstrating something about playing with ideas and also about using the therapist as an object of play. Both were using their therapist to relate in a new, unaccustomed, less conflictual way.

USE OF PLAY AND METAPHOR IN THE EARLY PHASE OF TREATMENT

Case Example

Six-year-old Mickey, presented in Chapter 5, described all the things he was afraid of in his first session. Among the distressing incidents of his life was the departure of his best friend, Sara, who had recently moved away.

Sara and Mickey reportedly spoke on the phone every day. Mickey said that they liked to solve mysteries together; this was their favorite activity. Sometimes, one child or the other would describe a new puzzle to solve, and the two would work together to figure it out.

Analysis

Mickey's therapist did not comment on Sara as this was only the first session. She decided from this narrative that Mickey did indeed miss Sara and that in some respects she was going to step into Sara's shoes—gumshoes—as a solver of mysteries and puzzles! The solving of psychological puzzles and mysteries would be the therapist's and Mickey's work together. This detective work was a metaphor for the psychotherapeutic efforts they would make to cure Mickey's psychological distress.

METAPHOR IN ONGOING TREATMENT

In later sessions, Mickey utilized that puzzle metaphor in many ways to symbolize a variety of symptoms. Mickey was panphobic, that is, phobic about a great many situations that caused him inordinate anxiety. Most of his fearfulness was focused around separations—going to school, leaving class to use the bathroom, trips, vacations, and so on. Mickey also had an eating disorder. He was fearful of trying new foods and restricted himself to three or four items that he could ingest (e.g., one type of dry cereal, chicken bits from a fast food restaurant, a specific brand of cookies).

After several months of treatment Mickey focused on a new game. He liked to play a game with his therapist that involved the creation of elaborately drawn mazes with a series of entrances and exits. The mazes sometimes took the form of a body with various orifices. Creating such a maze had the quality of an experiment; it was as if Mickey was attempting to figure out the maze of his own body. With his restricted food intake, Mickey was, needless to say, quite constipated and had painful bowel movements, which added to his fear of using the bathroom. In further sessions Mickey and his therapist discussed the processes of eating and elimination.

Mickey liked to design his mazes to be as complex as possible. He would then ask his therapist to make her way through them. He delighted in her becoming trapped in a dead-end part of a maze. At those times, she would playfully say to Mickey, "What will I do now? Will I ever see my family again? How will I ever find my way home?" or "Will I ever solve this puzzle?" Mickey assured her that she definitely would, but that it would take a long time. The therapist understood that Mickey wanted and would need to see her for a long time but that he also was expressing confidence in her ability to solve problems and to help him.

In one session the therapist commented that the maze that Mickey drew looked like a pregnant woman (the maze did indeed look like a woman on her back in labor.) She said that she thought he often wondered about the inside of his and other people's bodies and how they worked. Mickey commented that he remembered when his little sister was born. He said it was a long time ago (in actuality it had been three years). The therapist asked him to tell her about it. Mickey said that his father had awakened him at 5 in the morning to tell him. Mickey described his irritation at this, saying, "Why couldn't this wait until I woke up?" The therapist acknowledged his understandable irritation at being told he had a little sister (sibling rivalry).

Prior to her vacation, the therapist drew a maze with Mickey that involved travel over mountains, rivers, and valleys. Mickey picked out places to trap her ("A wizard will secretly be hiding behind a trap door and surprise you"). After each entrapment Mickey would then release his therapist. She commented that she knew he was nervous about travel. "Would you like me to send you postcards?" she asked him. Mickey said yes but he insisted that she only describe to him where she was exactly at that moment and not mention where she was going. The therapist accepted these terms and said it felt safer for Mickey to know exactly where she was. Mickey agreed and said that too many things could happen on your way to a place but that you could know and count on where you were at the moment.

Analysis

The travel game and its hazards might represent Mickey's anger at his therapist for abandoning him for a vacation, but it also represented Mickey's very real terrors of emotional separation and abandonment. The therapist agreed to utilize the postcards as a transitional object of herself to Mickey. He could remember her and hold on to these symbols of her until she returned. Mickey could then begin to master his separation anxiety via his transference to his social worker. She wrote the cards as Mickey requested (e.g., "I am now here looking at gondolas. I hope you're having a good time too"). When she returned, Mickey acknowledged receiving her cards and asked her to tell him more about where she had been, something she was glad to do. Only now could he allow himself to hear about and envision her travels.

THE TRANSITIONAL OBJECT AS METAPHOR

The great child analyst and theorist D. W. Winnicott conceived of the concept of the transitional object. The transitional object is the first "me, not me possession" and is a blanket or an important toy in a child's infancy or toddler phase. Its significance is that it creates the child's first illusion—that mother is present even if only in symbolic form. The transitional object, a much-loved toy or other object, helps the child maintain the comfort of mother's soothing presence.

In child therapy, there might be toys or objects in the therapy room that represent the therapist, something Greenson has called the transitional treatment object.

In the case of Mickey, the postcards functioned as transitional treatment objects. They served the purpose of maintaining a connection to his therapist during a potentially anxiety-producing situation.

CHAPTER 7

PSYCHOPATHOLOGY OF CHILDHOOD AND ADOLESCENCE

When children are brought to clinics and social agencies, they are foundering in their attempts at regulating behavior and affect. They are unable to play with spontaneity or learn without inhibition. Both self and object relations are impaired. A large spectrum of disorders in childhood emanates from experiences with abusive parental figures. Abuse includes physical trauma, sexual abuse, physical and emotional deprivation and neglect, and malnutrition (Fontana, 1971).

The childhood histories of abusing parents include a high frequency of deprivation, physical abuse, and scapegoating. Substance abuse, spouse abuse, and problematic work histories are frequently found to have been features of their families as well (Green, 1976).

It is clear that when family members are under inordinate multiple stressors, such as poverty, trauma, joblessness, housing problems, and racism, they are vulnerable to developing psychopathology and to continuing the cycle of abusive treatment of others.

Children suffer harm not only from acute physical and sexual abuse itself but also from the daily climate of pathology that exists in a family where extreme abuse is active. Green (1998) has chronicled the effect of punitive discipline, rough and chronically inappropriate handling, scapegoating, insensitivity, and cruelty present as a backdrop of everyday life. Children who experience early and unceasing rejection, abuse, and neglect are impaired in forming new relationships; they may approach them with fear and avoidance (Russ and Solomon, 1978). Such children frequently anticipate abuse from others. George and Main (1979) observed that abused toddlers avoided eye contact, are hypervigilant, and tend to approach their mothers from the side or rear, as if to avoid potential conflict.

Children who are abused learn to view violence and deprivation as a norm of relationships (Green, 1988). They may use the lower defenses, such as splitting, projection, denial, and grandiosity, to defend against their fears from perceived threats to their survival.

Abused children are easily frustrated and quick to express aggressive anger, responses that frequently culminate in such antisocial behavior as abuse of other children.

Abused children are also depressed and self-deprecating. Green (1976) reported that 40 percent of abused children in one study manifested overtly self-destructive behavior. Suicidal ideation may also be masked by violence to others.

S. Mitchell (1982) cited R. Shapiro's 1977 studies of families with severely disturbed adolescents. These families equated manifestations of separation-individuation with abandonment and attack. Adolescent family members not in agreement with this were perceived as being destructive and attacking (Shapiro, in Mitchell, 1982). Minuchin (1967), from a family systems perspective, described the enmeshed family as an "error activated" system, with the child's attempts at individuation being perceived as error by the rest of the system.

CONCEPTUALIZATIONS OF PATHOLOGY

In this chapter I outline two major categories of childhood disorders. Readers should bear in mind that the role of daily family life must be examined as an integral part of a child's life experience. Many of the disorders presented here are the result of abusive family scenarios; others are a response to some other aspect of life, such as illness or parental loss. Fairbairn (1941) described the psychopathologies as "techniques" of maintaining an early dyadic relationship, methods of organizing oneself around that relationship, of structuring it into the core of oneself and of seeking it everywhere, either in reality or by way of projection in one's perceptions of the world.

Kohut (1971) believed that the personality of the parental figure determined the result of the child's attempts to achieve a cohesive nuclear self. Tolpin (1971) pointed to disturbances of cohesion in child patients as being expressed in symptoms of free-floating anxiety, depression, rages, and an inability to learn new skills (Tolpin, in Elson, 1986).

Miriam Elson (1986) asserted that the fragmenting self in childhood may "sexualize needs and deficits," leading to enuresis, encopresis, compulsive masturbation, and precocious sexuality. She viewed all of these symptoms as compulsive attempts to fill in missing self-regulatory functions.

Self psychologists regard behavior that is driven and repetitive as an attempt to achieve recognition and mirroring from others. When children suffer self-fragmentation and loss of self-cohesion, the ego functions and defense mechanisms are affected. Their capacity for judgment, knowledge of consequences, choice of action, reality testing, and sublimation becomes impaired and is prevented from reaching development.

Relational theorists tend to see the borderline diagnosis and other preoedipal conditions as a result of an emotionally tr: childhood.

PSYCHOSES IN CHILDHOOD

Pervasive Developmental Disorders

In the past, childhood psychosis and childhood schizophrenia referred to children who exhibited the symptoms and impairments that today describe Pervasive Developmental Disorders (PDD). PDD is a conceptual umbrella for a number of specific disorders of childhood. PDD includes autism, childhood disintegration disorder, and Asperger's Disorder. Some PDD children emerge as schizophrenic in adulthood.

PDD is characterized by severe deficits in a number of areas of development, including social interaction and communication skills. Children with PDD display stereotyped behavior and may have abnormalities of the central nervous system.

Case Example: Asperger's Disorder

Sharra was the child of a schizophrenic mother and a drug-abusing father. When she was ten years old, she was diagnosed with Asperger's Disorder. Sharra scored in the superior range in IQ tests and had an extensive and sophisticated vocabulary. Nonetheless, her behavior was so disruptive that she became the scapegoat of other children (and of teachers who lacked an understanding of her disorder). Sharra would frequently stand up and wander around class when she was bored or anxious. She was often rigid in her behavior and would collapse into hysterical crying if she made a mistake. Inappropriate behavior erupted at important social events: when she forgot her lines in a class play, she had to be led off the stage sobbing; at a wedding she forgot the dance steps to a popular line dance and screamed for the group to start over again.

Kohut would have characterized this type of behavior as a primary disorder of the self. In this disorder, parental figures offer little consistent interest or happiness over the child's abilities and development. Although Sharra's difficulties had a congenital basis, she was also not adequately comforted and protected early on in life. She never received the kind of soothing responses that parental self-objects need to supply. As result, fragmentation was rapid for Sharra, as evidenced by her extreme behavior when her needs for perfection and the comfort of ritual were not met.

In Chapter 18, on special programs, I describe the type of school setting and program for children like Sharra.

Children with PDD often have a kind of charm. They utilize concrete thinking, that is, thinking that is primitive and bereft of abstract ability. Melanie Klein (1930) believed that the process of symbolic function begins to break down into concrete thought when anxiety becomes too great. In PDD this may be the case at times, but concrete thinking also may be a function of a neurological disorder.

Here is an illustration of concrete thinking, taken from the dialogue of two nine-year-olds with PDD:

MINDY: Look at my new shoes!
SAM: How pretty! Where did you get them?
MINDY: In the shoe store!

Mindy's telling of the obvious, rather than mentioning a specific shoe store or the circumstances that were involved in her receiving the shoes, is more typical of a three-year-old's cognitive level.

In addition to reflecting concrete thinking, Sharra's speech was often unrelated to the listener. She often gave long, impersonal, intellectual speeches as if she were giving a memorized lecture.

A testament to the skill of those involved in her treatment is that Sharra began to blossom when she was placed in a day school for children with PDD. Sharra went from class scapegoat (other children called her "the alien") to being elected class president. As her therapy progressed, she was able to become more appropriate and responsive in interpersonal situations and even demonstrated a new ability—a sense of humor. This requires not only an ability to utilize irony but also an ability to take distance from oneself; it also requires a less literal (i.e., less concrete) way of thinking. At times Sharra's therapist employed humorous responses to her so that the child could begin to move away from concrete thinking and develop a sense of perspective about herself and others. The prognosis for Sharra might be a good one if treatment can be kept consistent in her life.

Sharra's psychotherapy consisted of many components. At times her therapist had to clarify reality for Sharra by bringing reality to her frequently oscillating self states. This required using an empathic stance.

Empathic mirroring, a concept used in self psychology, affirms and validates the client's feelings and assists in regulating self states. This is akin to a parent comforting and explaining a confusing or distressing incident to a young child. Mirroring provides the missing components of self-esteem regulation.

At times the therapist or self-object must be a source of valida tion and confirmation of feelings, at other times a source of calm and protection. When the therapist is viewed as adversarial by the client, an opportunity is presented to work through, via transference, ruptures that took place in the past, that is, to teach the client new ways of relating to an object. The therapist becomes a conduit for multirational development, releasing the client from the more malignant bonds and ways of being from the past.

Borderline States

A borderline state is a phenomenological and descriptive concept of childhood pathology that is not used officially by the DSM-IV (the American Psychiatric Association's *Diagnostic and Statistical Manual of Mental Disorders,* 4th edition) for childhood disorders. The "official" diagnosis may be Conduct Disorder or some form of anxiety disorder. Borderline disorders refer to a wide range of difficulties in childhood. Children with a borderline personality organization have certain constellations of symptoms in common. Verhalst (in P. Kernberg, 1988) found the following symptoms in borderline children: primitive anxiety, primary process thinking, shifting levels of ego functioning, identity disturbance, primitive defense mechanisms, micro psychotic states, ineffective superego functioning, oddities of motor functioning, marked fantasy activity, and a discrepancy between talent and functioning in reality.

Paulina Kernberg (1988) noted that the behavior pattern that is characteristic of borderline children is a combination of both withdrawing and behavior that is "demanding, clinging and unpredictable."

The syndrome of Borderline Personality Disorder has been seen as a result of a failure of resolution of the separation-individuation phase of development. For borderline children, separation invokes intense levels of terror. Typically, borderline children either have experienced encouragement of excessive dependency from the primary parental figure or have been pushed toward a premature independence by a parent who is abandoning or lacking in concern. Sometimes both parental behaviors exist in the same parent. Indeed, inconsistency is often a characteristic of parents of borderline children.

The shifting pathological demands of their parents are reflected in borderline children's behavior. As one adolescent put it, "They want you to be president of the United States, but they won't let you cross the street alone!"

Some, though not all, children with this diagnosis require residential treatment. The latter is primarily a resource for children who are a danger to others or who are so fragile that remaining at home becomes a threat to their sanity.

Fred Pine (1974) noted that some children who exhibit psychotic behavior receive encouragement from their parents for this. For example, a child who describes hearing voices might be told, "That's nothing; I hear them too." Pine suggested that children in such an environment can benefit from a therapeutic community. Unfortunately, few residential facilities are staffed totally by enlightened, well-educated mental health workers.

Treatment that allows a child to be maintained in safety at home through the use of day programs and other community resources is infinitely preferable to the trauma of separation from family.

Case Example: A Borderline Child of an Alcoholic

Bruno, an aggressive ten-year-old boy, was referred to residential treatment because of severe antisocial and occasionally violent behavior. At the residence, Bruno was frequently obnoxious and continually critical of staff and other children. He seemed to be universally disliked. Although he could occasionally be charming, he seemed to be more invested in being as abusive as possible. His mother, Laureen, behaved similarly, both to Bruno and to staff members.

Bruno's behavior clearly was related to his mother's organizing principles. She was often demanding in her dealings with Bruno. She had, in the past, frequently exploited him by insisting that he babysit younger siblings for excessively long stretches of time, thus placing inappropriate responsibilities on the ten-year-old. Later on, as his treatment progressed, Bruno's trust in his therapist deepened sufficiently to allow him to tell her that his mother was frequently drunk to the point of passing out. He described his disgust at witnessing this. To the surprise of his therapist, he announced in a family session that if his mother ever did that again, he would ask that his weekend visit home be suspended. Bruno, perhaps more than other children in the residence, valued these visits more than anything else in his life; that he would voluntarily deny himself these visits in exchange for better treatment in life was a great move forward for him. His confronting Laureen was an act of personal courage.

Bruno really knew of no other way to relate to others than to be offensive. He related to others in the only way he knew how: by aggressively demanding to have his needs met and by reacting in an irritated and aggressive manner when they were left unmet.

From the beginning of his first sessions, Bruno made critical comments about his therapist. He complained that she had a lousy office, that she was feeding him lousy cookies, and so on. His therapist, aware of her dislike of Bruno, had to continually remind herself that the boy had himself been treated as he currently was treating her. This perspective enabled her to gain some control over herself and to avoid relating to him abusively in return. The therapy could only take place after the therapist proved she could tolerate Bruno's abuse and not be destroyed by it.

Case Example of Outpatient Treatment of a Borderline Child

Carola was an obese nine-year-old who lived with her mother and new stepfather. Her stepfather was considerably older than Carola's mother; indeed, in some respects, he acted as father to both mother and daughter. Carola received regular weekend visits from her father and his new wife (also considerably younger than her husband).

Both Carola's parents were narcissistic and self-involved. They loved Carola despite being excessively critical and demanding of her. Both parents, who were physically attractive people, were outspoken in their disappointment in Carola's obesity. Carola's school reports indicated that she was having behavioral difficulties. She was occasionally disruptive and was often teased by other children. She reportedly had no friends and described herself as lonely. She routinely blamed the other children for fights that she reportedly started.

In sessions, Carola revealed her fantasies about her life at home: she talked of living in an enormous apartment and of her mother and stepfather owning a limousine and a Jacuzzi whirlpool bath (none of this was true). Paulina Kernberg (1988) noted that the play of borderline children has a "compulsive, static" quality, even in fantasy. It is useful to apply Winnicott's concept of the true and false self here as well: when a high degree of spontaneity of one's true self has been abandoned to complying with the needs of others, a sacrifice of individuality and creativity is made (Winnicott, 1960). Winnicott noted that lying is a sign of a false self. Carola lied to impress the therapist but sacrificed the truth of her own experience to do so. The cost of autonomy is a high price to pay if loss of an important relationship is the price tag.

Carola's compulsive eating can be viewed as an attempt to maintain self-cohesion; she ate to regulate her constant anxiety. Her sense of not being good enough physically to please her very narcissistic and unnuturing parents was, understandably, a source of terror for her. In addition, she represented to her parents a target on which to focus their complaints and unhappiness in life. As a problem child, Carola deflected her parents' conflicts onto herself. She became their projection of her as bad. Carola's mother described herself as fat as a child. Her rages and criticism of Carola were often expressions of her own self-hatred; she viewed Carola as a "part object," that is, as an extension of herself via projection. This implies a lack of differentiation in the way Carola's mother saw her. (Carola's father also saw her as an extension of her mother, the woman who had left him years earlier.) The therapist was struck by how Carola's weight-conscious mother often supplied her daughter with excessive amounts of food, even when food wasn't requested. It seemed to the therapist that Carola was being fed to silence her so that she wouldn't make any further demands upon her mother. Chodorow (1978) noted that boundaries between mothers and daughters often tend to be very permeable and easily violated. Carola felt significantly unheard and was overfed to stifle her complaints. Her weight kept her dependent on her mother and kept her mother continually engaged with her (albeit in a negative way).

Family Therapy with Borderline Children

Both Bruno and Carola benefited from conjoint family sessions to some degree. Eventually, Bruno's mother requested ongoing treatment for herself with Bruno's therapist. It was important to her that Bruno's therapist conduct the treatment; she had never been able to make a connection to a therapist before. As a result of seeing both mother and child, the therapist was able to work more actively in integrating important factors that affected both clients. For example, in one family session, Bruno was able, with his therapist's support, to confront his mother with her substance abuse for the first time. The therapist could then go on to help Bruno's mother understand how Bruno was feeling.

In Carola's case, all four parents and stepparents attended a family session. They needed to hear about the girl's despair. It was clear that in their constant need to argue they had not recognized Carola's conflicted sense of loyalty at hearing each parent criticize the other.

It is a great sense of relief to children to have an adult, the therapist, intervene on their behalf, either as an advocate for better treatment from parental figures or as one who can explain to parents something of their child's inner life.

Siskind (1997) has noted that when a parent seeks treatment with her child's therapist, the latter is able to view that parent in the context of her own life. This is especially important when the parent is additionally overburdened with the stress of being a single parent (Chodorow, 1978).

CHAPTER 8

POSTTRAUMATIC STRESS DISORDER

J. Herman (1992) believes that survivors of trauma exhibit symptoms similar to borderline and other personality disorders, although the etiology of the disorders is different. Like people diagnosed with borderline personality disorders, trauma survivors show symptoms of chronic anxiety, chronic depression (including suicidal gestures), low self-esteem, somatic complaints, impulsivity and interpersonal problems.

There is a high correlation between a diagnosis of Borderline Personality Disorder in adolescent inpatients and a history of sexual or physical abuse. Herman (1985) found that one-third of female outpatients experienced abuse, with 13 percent of this group experiencing sexual abuse. Bryer (1987) found that 72 percent of female inpatient adolescents experienced a history of abuse.

SEQUELAE OF POSTTRAUMATIC STRESS DISORDER

Posttraumatic Stress Disorder (PTSD) has a more permanent influence over adulthood if the trauma occurred before or during the latency period. In this disorder, basic physchological processes are affected. These include self-esteem, identity, regulation of affects, reality testing, expectation of relationships, trust, strategies for achieving goals, and cognitive functioning.

It is important to recognize the impact of trauma on cognition; cognitive disruptions from trauma often are diagnosed as learning disabilities. The cognitive sequelae of trauma may involve inhibition and constriction of thought; an inflexible and hysterical cognitive style that impedes logical, analytical thinking; an inability to plan, utilize self-observation, and perspective; and a lack of ability to focus attention or to employ disciplined concentration (Western et al., 1990).

The symptoms that are basic both to adolescents who have experienced severe abuse and to those diagnosed as borderline are suicide attempts, depression, behavioral disturbances, and running away.

Since borderline adolescents tend to have a history of abuse by multiple perpetrators, it is believed that physical and, especially, sexual abuse play a major role in the etiology of Borderline Personality Disorder in adolescence.

Terr (1983), Herman (1985), Finkelhor (1984), and VanderKolk (1987) have all described the following characteristics of those who have suffered childhood trauma: strongly visualized memories, repetitive behavior, trauma-specific fears (e.g., fear of the dark if the trauma occurred at night), and sudden changed attitudes about people, life, and the future (i.e., illusions and assumptions about people and the world as good and meaningful are shattered). It is important to remember that some illusions about life are important as defenses. In his memoir *Night,* Elie Wiesel described his experience of Auschwitz as an adolescent; he said that the Nazis had not only destroyed his family but also his belief in God.

PLAY THERAPY IN POSTTRAUMATIC STRESS DISORDER

Lenore Terr (1983) identified the characteristics of play reflecting posttraumatic stress. Among the characteristics are compulsive repetition, an unconscious link between play and traumatic event, literal or concrete play, lack of lessening anxiety, the presence of danger, and fears of contagion from other children. Terr emphasized the monotony of the traumatized child's ritualized play and the quality of secrecy involved (i.e., the play takes place in some fantasized hidden arena, such as underground). The monotony of the ritual play of traumatized children described by Terr is much like the ritual of sadomasochistic scenarios that adult survivors of abuse occasionally engage in.

Social work practice today includes more work with traumatized clients than ever before. Most child guidance agency cases are, in some respect, cases of Posttraumatic Stress Disorder. This diagnosis is a wide-ranging one. According to DSM-IV, traumatic stress is an anxiety disorder. Essential to a diagnosis of this disorder is a series of symptoms that are the sequelae to experiencing an extreme traumatic stressor. The stressor can be physical or sexual abuse, experiencing or witnessing death, extreme violence, and threats to the physical integrity of the self or such threats to loved ones or close associates. Living through a war or through a natural disaster, such as an earthquake or flood, is included in PTSD. For children, the repeated experience of trauma at the hands of an adult forces them to organize their very personality around the abuser, especially if this is someone close to them or very important to them. The sequelae of the child's repeated exposure to violence, physical and extreme emotional abuse, and sexual abuse are especially pronounced in the area of cognitive development. If the abuse began in infancy and continued through early childhood, the residual effects on the psyche and on cognition will almost always be considerable. Cognitive disruption may appear as an inhibition to intellectual learning. Signs of such disruption are as follows: inability to pay attention or concentrate, inability to follow or bring a sentence or evaluation to its logical conclusion, labile affect, distortion of perception, loose or tangential thought, inhibition of curiosity, self-destructive behavior, impulsive behavior, inability to modulate affect, and somatic symptoms.

There is a profound sense of shame in physically and sexually abused children. There is also a lack of hope, a loss of the sense of the goodness of life. There is often a lack of belief in relationships being worth investing in. PTSD victims sometimes resort to manipulation to gain a goal. Some children report repeated nightmares and have specific fears or phobias associated with the initial abuse (e.g., fears of the dark, of closets, or other associations with fear experienced during abuse).

Example

A child who had been tortured by an older sibling by being locked in a closet might experience fears of opening doors or putting things away in closets. Some children will repeat trauma in play. By way of repetition compulsion, they attempt to master the earliest dread and anxiety associated with trauma.

Case Example: Rolando

At age six, Rolando had been found abandoned with his other siblings and removed to the county hospital (as described in Chapter 14, on foster care). He and his siblings were covered with cigarette burns and were described as wild beyond the experience of the hospital staff.

By age six, Rolando had witnessed his father murdering his wife's lover, had been physically abused and possibly starved. After the hospital, he was brought to residential treatment. Initially, his behavior looked very much like an attention-deficit disorder, with extreme hyperactivity.

Rolando was also a very engaging and good-looking child. He often used his cuteness to manipulate staff and was periodically competitive and provocative to other children, who usually disliked him.

After about a year of treatment, Rolando felt comfortable enough with his therapist to initiate a very repetitive form of play. Routinely, his therapist would pick Rolando up from class and bring him to her office. Rolando would begin to run from her to hide somewhere quite near her office. The therapist would then pretend to look for him. Rolando seemed to enjoy her (pretend) distress and loved being found by her. The therapist would enthusiastically exclaim, "Oh, Rolando! I'm so glad I found you!" Rolando would then enter the therapy room and initiate a game. This game involved a man breaking into the session and committing a murder. Sometimes the therapist was murdered; at other times, Rolando asked her to play the murderer. After weeks of this, the therapist, in consultation with her supervisor, felt ready to comment and interpret this play. The next time Rolando initiated the murder scenario, the social worker said, "I can see that this is something you are very concerned with, Rolando. I have some information that may be helpful to you. Would you like to hear it?"

Rolando put down his toys, looked her in the eye, and said, "Yes, I do."

The therapist then explained that the staff believed that he and his siblings had witnessed a murder, that his father had killed his mother's boyfriend. She said that this must have been a very frightening experience for Rolando and his brothers and sisters. Rolando, noticeably calmer, began to question his social worker: When had this happened? What had his siblings done? And so on. She explained to the best of her ability that his father had been arrested and was currently in jail. His mother, although alive, had disappeared after a while for fear of arrest for abusing the children. (This latter information about his mother had already been discussed with Rolando.)

After the session, the child care staff was alerted to the fact that Rolando might need to continue to talk about the details he had just learned. He continued to discuss them with everyone for a very long time. VanderKolk (1989) described the need to compulsively repeat and reenact trauma as a component of PTSD.

In terms of her own countertransference, the worker was understandably terrified of discussing the murder directly with Rolando. In part, she feared reintroducing this terrifying memory to a young child. She noted however, that after this disclosure, Rolando no longer needed to play out the murder scenario. He now needed to talk about his father, the murder, and his mother's abuse and subsequent abandonment of him.

Most sessions with PTSD children are not as cathartic as this one. The therapeutic work with traumatized children is long and often excruciating to listen to. It is important that the therapist overcome fears of hearing the often torturous accounts of trauma. If this cannot happen, the child is reaffirmed in the idea that it is he or she who is bad and shameful, and a collusion takes place between child and therapist: that this is forbidden material to discuss.

An Outpatient Management of PTSD in an Adolescent Girl

Tricia, a pretty, overweight, sixteen-year-old girl had been removed from the custody of her mother and stepfather. They resided in another state. Tricia had reported her stepfather's attempts to sexually molest her to protective services. He had also abused her two younger sisters. Unfortunately, the family moved to another state before all the children could be removed to safety. Tricia stayed in touch with her sisters but was sickened over their welfare. She currently lived with grandparents, who were loving and sympathetic to her. Tricia had become an aggressive, argumentative girl. She frequently was fearless in engaging needlessly with more violently aggressive girls in her school. She often challenged these girls to rapping contests—rhyming hostile or abusive lyrics that were inventive but provocative to others.

Tricia liked her social worker and began to confide more in her. Tricia would pick up men who were delivery men, cab drivers, maintenance employees, and so on, from her urban neighborhood. She described bringing them to an abandoned building near her home to have sex. Her sexual contacts were unprotected by safe sex methods, and she gave no thought to birth control. As Tricia put it, "I fuck them before they can fuck me."

Analysis

Tricia was clearly identified with the aggressor, a common phenomenon in those victimized by sexual or physical abuse. By engaging in daredevil behavior, she invited danger and further abuse, but Tricia was operating from a grandiose fantasy: that she was in total control and would never be abused again. From another perspective, she continued the kind of bad object attachment described in Chapter 2. By picking up men in service-related employment, she could feel contempt and disdain for their lower economic status.

The therapist pointed out Tricia's identification with her stepfather. She said that even though Tricia hated him, she seemed to be modeling herself after him by being the aggressor. This might help her in one way to feel more powerful, her therapist told her, but fundamentally put her at terrible risk; she was, in effect, still feeling possessed by her stepfather, although now this was internalized. Tricia could hear this but continued her behavior; by now, it had become truly compulsive. The therapist asked her if she ever thought of therapy during these sexual encounters or even when she challenged the tougher girls at school. The therapist told her that if treatment was to work, Tricia needed to think about it more actively, especially when she initiated a dangerous scenario.

A concern in treating adolescents engaged in this kind of risky behavior is that they might contract a sexually transmitted disease or be hurt in some violent altercation. Rules about reporting this kind of at-risk behavior to parents vary from state to state. Because Tricia was a minor, her therapist had to inform her guardians that she could neither control Tricia's at-risk behavior nor protect her. The therapist told the guardians that she was quite willing to continue treatment but that they needed to be apprised of risks Tricia was taking.

The therapist told Tricia of her need to discuss her behavior with her guardians. At first Tricia was angry that the therapist had betrayed her trust by divulging confidential information to others. The therapist agreed that Tricia's anger was justified. She pointed out that in the past Tricia had complained that no one had adequately protected her and her sisters. The therapist said that by warning her guardians she was attempting to protect her and, in addition, was being ethical by following a law designed to protect children. Tricia was finally able to accept the fact that her therapist was trying to protect her.

Unfortunately, social workers all too often face case difficulties like Rolando's and Tricia's. Whether in the inner city or in suburban or rural communities, working with trauma is the greatest challenge to turning around a child's life.

DISSOCIATIVE STATES

Dissociation is possibly the most extreme manifestation of trauma. The DSM-IV describes Dissociative Identity Disorder (formerly called Multiple Personality Disorder) as the existence of two or more distinct personalities within the self. These personality states alternate and take full control of the person's behavior. Some dissociative states include Dissociative Fugue (formerly Psychogenic Fugue), characterized by sudden, unexpected travel with an inability to remember one's past, the assumption of a new identity, or episodes of amnesia (inability to recall important personal information).

Dissociation is an attempt by the psyche to disavow trauma to the self that may be unspeakable or unbearable and threatening to the cohesion of the psyche. In a dissociative state, the individual's experience of consciousness is split and the traumatic experience itself is disavowed or split off, establishing a separate psychic state within the self.

The following case illustrates a dissociative state in late adolescence as a result of early sexual abuse.

Case Example

Susan described a history of incest with her father. This began in early childhood and continued over a number of years. It was one of the most horrendous cases of sexual abuse that this therapist had ever encountered. The client attempted to tell a neighbor about the abuse. It is significant that she chose someone who was both senile and alcoholic and who would not help her.

In many trauma cases, the normal level of mistrust that one should experience for self-protection is lowered or nonexistent (Herman, 1992). This enables a replication of the original trauma or violation to occur. Susan had an idealized view of her therapist. Susan admired her therapist and thought she was a high-class lady who had never known what it is like to suffer. These beliefs enabled Susan to experience her therapist as calming, infallible, and omnipotent— that is, beyond attack while she remained dirty and sullied.

The patient had now organized the therapeutic relationship in an intriguing way: in order to maintain a relationship to a beloved ideal figure, her therapist, she needed to keep herself debased so as to relate to a powerful, idealized other.

Susan recounted the following memory: After one horrific episode, in which her father threatened to sell her into prostitution to pay off his gambling debts, Susan described herself as "going dead." She then developed an alternative self: a young male teacher whom she, in reality, idealized. In her dissociative state, Susan described how she truly became the teacher; she now walked and talked like him and adopted his name. She felt that now she, as the teacher for whom she named herself, could relate to her therapist as the kind of man who is good to women. Indeed, she felt that she now could relate to others as well as her therapist as an equal.

Analysis and Intervention

The therapist had to work hard to help Susan reintegrate the "dirty, sullied" part of herself. With great compassion, she identified (over a long time) her client's hatred of feeling helpless and vulnerable to her father's vicious, torturous attacks. As the charming male teacher, the client could somehow be an equal, a peer, to contend with, as opposed to feeling helpless. In helping Susan to reintegrate the disavowed aspect of herself as a victim of abuse, the therapist needed to listen patiently to all of Susan's fantasies as they related to her within the context of the transference. The therapist knew that in order to hear as much of Susan's story as possible, it was important to allow Susan to feel free to express her fantasies.

In exploring her client's fantasies, the therapist became a witness to Susan's inner world. She knew that she would be able to help her to integrate a self-identity much more readily than if she were to forbid further expression of this fantasy life. Over a period of two years, Susan was, in fact, able to give up her dissociative alter self and own her better-integrated own psyche again.

By utilizing a relational treatment model with PTSD, therapists can expect to work with a variety of manifestations of the trauma: enactments via the transference, residual sequelae of the trauma itself, disturbed internalized object relations and the concomitant fantasies and expectations of interpersonal relationships.

Together, client and therapist can discover and clarify the meaning of the client's experience. Davies and Frawley (1994) emphasized the importance of the therapist's active verbal participation and observation in the course of treatment.

Many patients who have experienced sexual abuse repeat the trauma in their interpersonal relationships. These may be bad relationships in reality, or the negative aspects may be the product of projections by the client. These projections are, in a sense, an expectation based upon historical reality.

In the previous example, the client saw her therapist as ideal and lofty, and herself as sullied and dirty. She needed to preserve her therapist as a source of goodness, at least in fantasy, in order to remain in the relationship. She had learned to structure herself and her relationships around her sexual trauma and the expectation of further abuse. By keeping herself "debased," she was at least able to retain a relationship with a more powerful other—in the transference, an ideal other who became bigger than life. The need to see one's objects as overly important and as having greater needs than oneself is a paradigm common to people who have had early abusive relationships. Fairbairn (1954) noted that in the relationships of hysterics the object of fantasy is always overendowed with importance; overvalued, while the needs of the subject seem more and more diminished. Hysterics often react in an extreme manner to loss. Freud's famous quote on depression—"The shadow of the object falls upon the ego"—is relevant here; the shadow of the object not only colors the affect of the ego but looms in enormity over it. In this case example, the client played this out in the transference. In her fantasy she believed that if only she were an empowered man, she would then be an equal to her therapist, as well as loved by her. This paradigm of relationship was to be played out by this client many times. As treatment progressed, Susan left her dissociative fantasy state behind, but she continued to exhibit a large degree of identification with the aggressor. She did so by acting out the part of dominatrix with men

whom she could control and dominate but who also were more benign than her abusive father.

POSTTRAUMATIC STRESS DISORDER IN FAMILY TREATMENT

Cara was the six-year-old only child of a single mother, Mrs. Atkins.
Mrs. Atkins had brought Cara to treatment because Cara had recently told her she was being sexually abused by the husband of a
next-door neighbor. The neighbor had since moved away but occasionally had offered to baby-sit for Cara. Additionally, Cara's behavior had become hyperactive in school, probably as a result of the
sexual abuse. Mrs. Atkins worked in an office during the day and was
beset by guilt at having left Cara with someone who would abuse
her. Both Mrs. Atkins and Cara saw the therapist individually and
also had conjoint family sessions.

Mrs. Atkins, a soft-spoken woman, was a loving and attentive
mother with little support from her family of origin; she had estranged herself from her family in adolescence. Mrs. Atkins also described having been sexually abused by a cousin who lived with her
family. The family blamed her when she attempted to disclose this
information, and she had left home shortly thereafter.

Cara described being fondled several times by the next-door
neighbor's husband but described no further assault. She had, however, wanted to tell her mother about the abuse, feeling guilty and
bad for having experienced it, as if she had somehow elicited the
neighbor's abuse.

Many victims of sexual abuse describe a pervasive feeling of
shame. It is as if they believe that they somehow have made it happen. Sometimes, perpetrators of abuse will tell the victim this—that
it is the victim who has brought the abuse upon herself by being
"bad," "provocative," and so forth.

Mrs. Atkins, too, felt guilt and shame. Rationally, she knew that she had to work to give Cara and herself a decent life but felt like an abandoning, uncaring mother (something like her own family's attitude toward her as a child). Mrs. Atkins described many of the feelings that working mothers typically have about having to leave strangers in charge of their children. In addition, she felt a return of the old feelings of shame at the sexual abuse that she herself had endured as an adolescent.

Mrs. Atkins's concern was to let Cara know that she did indeed love her. She wanted Cara to know that in the future she should come to her immediately if such abuse should ever happen again. The therapist suggested a joint session. Mrs. Atkins had felt unable to do this for fear of breaking down in front of her daughter. The therapist here suggested that Mrs. Atkins knew her daughter better than anyone and loved her better than anyone. The therapist thought that if Mrs. Atkins could start to talk to Cara about what had happened, they could build on their relationship so that Cara could begin to feel comforted and see her mother as a source of protection as well as nurturance. The therapist acknowledged to Mrs. Atkins that she would be there to facilitate this.

The meeting took place, and Cara was able to describe what had happened with the neighbor and her fears of disappointing her mother. Mrs. Atkins was then able to comfort her daughter and assure her that what had happened was not her fault. As both began to cry, the therapist suggested that Cara go to her mother for comfort. Mrs. Atkins was happy to embrace her daughter and held her on her lap while they talked about how Cara needed to feel safe again and needed to come to her mother whenever she felt fearful of others.

VanderKolk (1993) has described the excruciating pain that a parent feels in thinking of her child's experience of abuse. Mrs. Atkins's sense of helplessness and guilt, the lack of decent available child care versus the demands of work, added to her sense of guilt about somehow neglecting her daughter.

The frustration and cruelty of this situation are what many single parents face when torn between responsible caregiving for a child and the pressure of having to work at the same time. This poses a very real dilemma for single mothers. It is important that the social worker validate the reality of any situation before exploring intrapsychic conflicts or responses to any situation.

In work with trauma, theorists have suggested that the final phase of treatment examine feelings about oneself (self representation) and relational development. In particular, the ability to reconnect despite the sequelae of trauma that affect relationships is crucial (Herman, 1992). Mrs. Atkins needed to rebuild her damaged sense of trust and vulnerability in relationships. At the same time, she needed to reestablish herself as the primary source of comfort to Cara so that Cara could view her mother in turn as a dependable source of nurturance and protection.

CHAPTER 9

LEARNING DISABILITIES

Any assessment of learning disabilities should be done in conjunction with psychological testing, which can assist in diagnosing specific cognitive difficulties, learning disabilities, and other neurological deficits.

Attention Deficit Disorder with Hyperactivity (ADHD) has its origins in both genetic and environmental sources. Children with this diagnosis display inappropriate behavior for their age, accompanied by hyperactivity, impulsivity, and an inability to concentrate. Most children are referred between ages eight and ten (Hunt, 1988).

Symptoms associated with this diagnosis include frequent fidgeting, difficulty remaining seated, distractibility, difficulty waiting for one's turn, blurting out answers to questions prematurely, difficulty following through on instructions, difficulty sustaining attention, shifting from one incomplete activity to another, difficulty playing quietly, frequently intruding upon others, losing things frequently, and engaging in dangerous behavior without regard for possible consequences (DSM-IV). Many of these symptoms can be attributed to a wide variety of causes. For example, Posttraumatic Stress Disorder is one common link to ADHD, and minimal brain dysfunction occasionally follows head trauma or illness (Rutter, in Hunt, 1982).

Children with an ADHD diagnosis often suffer from low self-esteem, for they are frequently punished in school and at home for behavior that they cannot control. They may also become depressed. S. Escalona has described how children with ADHD know what they are supposed to do and feel bad when they cannot do it. Just as adults know that they are supposed to work, children understand that they are supposed to do well at school (S. Escalona, unpublished lecture).

Even when children with ADHD do well as a result of supplemental tutoring, they may find that tutoring is still needed in adolescence. High school, with the need to change class for every subject and the more abstract concepts in the course work, may provoke disorganized behavior regarding learning. This coupled with the normal stressors of adolescence may put the ADHD adolescent at risk for acting out behavior and substance abuse.

TREATMENT ISSUES IN WORKING WITH ADHD AND HYPERACTIVITY

It is helpful in the treatment of hyperactive children to have a less stimulating office environment. To minimize the element of distractibility in hyperactive children, the therapist may want to put away toys and games that are normally left out. To minimize the degree to which a hyperactive child may become overwhelmed and disorganized by a chaotic environment, the therapist might suggest taking out one toy or game at a time and putting it away before taking out another.

Depending on the severity of the child's learning disability, the therapist can use simple, clear, and uncomplicated sentences when speaking with the child. Consideration should also be given to the need for tutoring and remediation.

The families of children with learning disabilities often experience the child's difficulties as a narcissistic injury.

SPECIAL PROGRAMS AND ADHD

Many after-school community-based programs now offer special services, from tutoring to group activities, for ADHD children. The following vignette illustrates the ego-enhancing possibilities offered by a Cub Scout pack designed specifically for boys with severe ADHD symptoms.

Case Example

The boys were paying unusual attention to one member who was displaying the different badges that the scouts could earn as they advanced through the program. The group leader described the different levels of attainment for badges while the group member displayed his "wolf" badge. The group was unusually attentive and clearly entranced by this talk. It was clear that they were excited and invested in advancement. They were able to focus and pay attention to a process that was ego-enhancing and that enabled the group to bond together with pride.

Part II

THE
MIDDLE
PHASE
of
TREATMENT

CHAPTER 10

TRANSFERENCE

L ewis Aron (1996) has written of the need for mutuality between therapist and patient as reflective of the child's earliest involvement with parental figures.

Children are attentive to their parents' personalities. They can imagine and become responsive to and engrossed (in fantasy or reality) in what their parents are absorbed by. Recall the case of Mickey, introduced in Chapter 5. Mickey wanted his mother to love the things his father loved—baseball cards. He reasoned that the concerns and preoccupations of his parents could be resolved if some mutuality of their wishes and desires could be brought about.

Children's concerns, conscious and unconscious, are reflected in the treatment arena. Children often project onto the therapist their experience of reality. In a sense, they continue to see adults as similar to their parents. It makes sense that a child would assume that all adults behave in the same way.

Some children, however, are also deeply concerned to protect the therapist from knowing about the therapist's flaws, protecting the therapist from anger that might shatter the therapist's grandiosity. These children need to use themselves as grandiose self-objects, that is, as mirroring back the therapist's grandiosity. Such children, often from single-parent households, may have performed this function for the parent. Children of alcoholics and of deeply depressed parents also frequently perform this function. They need to cheer and comfort the parent at the expense of their own needs for comforting, solace, and a sense of tranquillity. Often this interactional pattern appears in the form of idealizing the therapist throughout the early middle phases and late phases of treatment.

IDEALIZATION IN THE TRANSFERENCE IN THE MIDDLE PHASE OF TREATMENT

Case Example

Janie, a nine-year-old, described consistent unfairness in her family. Her father openly favored his son over Janie. He was also quite demeaning of his wife, Janie's mother, who did little to defend herself and, in fact, often agreed with her husband's disparaging remarks of her character. Janie said she felt that in her family there were two teams, "the boys and the girls," and that "the girls always lost."

Janie idealized her therapist, however, always seeing her in the most flattering light. One day she admired the therapist's clothes, commenting, "You're all in velvet and suede today." Janie wrote a story about the therapist and herself. She described their adventures and close friendship. In the story, boys pursued them but Janie and her therapist disdainfully eschewed contact with them, telling them, "Go away, you stupid, idiotic idiots." In her idealization of the therapist, Janie felt attached and somewhat merged with an admirable and powerful female figure: the two of them escape and disdain the men.

Curiously, Janie's father and mother also idealized the therapist, seeing her as "a sophisticated woman of the world who could throw away the textbooks." (The therapist herself felt irritated by the parents' excessive and fawning flattery and angered by their emotional abuse of their child.) Both husband and wife described having narcissistic parents who were often neglectful of them and who required a great deal of flattering from them.

Both Janie and her parents were organizing themselves in treatment around the perceived needs of the therapist as authority figure: their idealization of the therapist served to make them feel more valuable in turn.

THE TRANSFERENCE AS COMMUNICATION

How the therapist is perceived by the child in treatment needs to be understood as a communication. Sometimes, the child's transference reflects a deficit in the self: what Kohut termed a lack of sufficient mirroring back of archaic (early) grandiose impulses. Sometimes, the lack reflects the parent's failure as a source of potential safety and protection and as a source of admiration in representing ideals. The transference often reflects the kind of "bad object" projection that Fairbairn wrote about. This too is a means of relating and of keeping a certain kind of object present, because it is deeply familiar (and is also the only known source of love and reality). This is a way of structuring the familiar into one's own self-experience and into the context of relational experiences.

Case Example

An abused child living in the South Bronx described his pet dog to his idealized therapist. The dog was a pit bull and had been trained by adults to be even more ferocious so as to fight in dog fights for gamblers in the neighborhood. The dog had been taught to tear into other dogs by mutilating them in the genital area. The child was ecstatic as he described how the dog had severed the testicles of another dog in a fight and then come to him, wagging his tail, for approval. The child's eyes glowed as he told his social worker that the dog came to him for love ("He wanted my love") and offered his gruesome sacrifice for the child's approval.

In this example, the therapist is protected by idealization and is safe enough for the child to be able to relate the story of the dog and his way of seeking love and approval. The therapist can mirror and validate the child's perception of his importance to his dog.

THE DEVELOPMENT OF TRANSFERENCE

For the purposes of teaching, I give many case examples throughout this book that utilize the therapist's interpretations. I do not wish to give the impression that every action needs a comment in child therapy. Far from that, I am countering something I have observed in American child therapy over the last twenty years, namely, that many child therapists say nothing at all.

Winnicott spoke of the danger of the therapist interpreting too much. By being overly interpretive, the therapist cuts short the patient's "ability to creatively discover." The therapist becomes dangerous for "knowing too much, too in communication with the still and silent spot of the patient's ego organization" (Winnicott, unpublished, cited in Phillips, 1988). Adam Phillips (1988) commented that "language in this context is a potentially terrifying maternal object, i.e., the over-interpretive analyst becomes the tyrannical mother and language is integral to her power."

In the following case, the transference and its relationship to language was of primary importance.

Case Example

Early Phase of Treatment
Milena, age eleven, had been an electively mute child in residential treatment for two years before returning home. She had previously lived alone with her mother, a very depressed, isolated young woman. Her mother had little help or financial assistance. She often

spent hours in silence with Milena, who had become increasingly isolated. Sometimes Milena would wander the streets for hours, following her mother's demand that she go out and make friends.

After her stay in the residence, Milena spoke more frequently than before, but her speech was still limited. She then began outpatient therapy at age thirteen, but she complained that the therapist didn't talk enough and that she had nothing to say.

The therapist asked if it would help if she spoke. Milena said it would. The therapist invited Milena to ask her questions, because, as Milena well knew, it was hard to speak without knowing what to talk about.

Milena agreed and proceeded to ask the therapist questions— about what she did all week and on weekends; where she went; what she did or saw; what restaurants she ate in with her husband; what the food was like, the wine, the movie; what clothes she wore. These questions were repeated monotonously and plaintively week after week, with a childlike curiosity. The therapist tried her best to answer these questions, thinking first about what could be told and what shouldn't be told. For a long time, Milena did not speak about herself. The therapist felt herself very much "used as an object," in Winnicott's sense; she felt that she was demonstrating to a very young child how to have a relationship.

Middle Phase of Treatment

After one year, Milena suddenly changed. She picked up an inexpensive fountain pen belonging to the therapist and asked its price. After being told "seven dollars," she exclaimed, "You spent seven dollars on a pen? What kind of extravagant idiot are you? All you do is go out, wear fancy clothes, and eat in restaurants. What kind of brainless person are you?"

The transference had now changed; from a quasi-idealized selfobject, the therapist had now become a devalued, frivolous fool. At home Milena began to complain to her mother, "How come we never go places or do anything like my therapist does?"

The projections clearly shifted. This was an important pivotal moment in the treatment process. The therapist, who had felt very much like a false self before, felt very real now. She encouraged Milena to tell her more, and this request inaugurated a period of verbal abuse from the client. The therapist alternately listened and responded (sometimes good-naturedly exclaiming, "You think I'm *that* bad?" so that her client could feel safe in continuing her invective). Milena continued to complain that the therapist didn't talk enough, but she also occasionally (begrudgingly) said to her, "At least you talk sometimes."

Winnicott pointed out that therapists need to ask themselves, "Who am I representing? What am I being used to do?" Phillips (1988) said that the patient is always "trying to go somewhere . . . via the analyst," and that "interpretations are passports."

Christopher Bollas (1987), reflecting on his work with nonverbal autistic and schizophrenic children, noted that if therapists are willing to be "used as an object" and "to be guided via [their] own internal world," they will also discover the patient's memory of early object relations. Following Paula Heimann, Bollas suggested that therapists ask themselves, "To whom is this patient speaking (now)? What is the patient talking about and why now?" Adding to this, Margaret Little commented that therapists should ask themselves how they are feeling, why they are feeling this and why now, in order to examine their own countertransference feelings. To this advice, Bollas (1987) added Bion's suggestion to therapists to ask themselves the question "What is speaking, or transpiring, in what form and linked to what?"

All of these writers recognize that the transference is directly tied to the countertransference. For example, Milena could only begin to utilize her therapist after she realized that the therapist could accept her noncommunicativeness and her need to utilize the therapist as an object of curiosity (as a new person for relating in her realm of experience). Milena could then discover new ways of relating to an adult, differently from her earlier style of relating. In the past, she viewed the therapist as similar to her mother. Milena could utilize the therapist still more when the therapist accepted her rejecting verbalizations. Milena needed to maintain what Fairbairn has termed a "closed system" relationship, that is, a continuation of old ways of relating to familiar objects.

An attempt on the therapist's part at relating too quickly would have thwarted the therapeutic work. Milena could not have tolerated this; it would have felt engulfing and terrifying. Seinfeld (1990) has suggested that some borderline children experience the therapist's attempts to be helpful as engulfing; it is only when the therapist is willing to accept the child's rejecting relatedness that the therapist can begin to be internalized. This internalization will be reflected in a slow shift as the child becomes more benign to herself and to the therapist.

Late Phase of Treatment

Later on in treatment, Milena began to connect herself to the therapist via a transitional object. She took some cuttings of a plant in the therapist's office, carefully placing the cuttings in water in an apple-shaped juice jar the therapist had. Milena commented that these plants would be the children and grandchildren of the therapist's plants; their vines reminded her "of long arms" and of the therapist, who had long hair. Since these cuttings were taken before the therapist's vacation, they functioned for Milena as a transitional tie to the therapist while she was away.

Throughout this book I have referred to Winnicott's concept of the transitional object. Recall that the transitional object represents the illusion to the infant that the mother's comfort is still present. In Milena's case, the plant cuttings served as a constant object representation of the therapist in a concrete form. By looking at the new plants and keeping them alive, she could keep alive the therapeutic relationship (for many borderline patients, separation is equivalent to abandonment and annihilation). The plants became extensions of the therapist herself, their tendrils as long arms, representing contact and connectedness. In another sense, the new plants also represented an extension of Milena in her newfound self, which was emerging with the creative ability to play and to speak.

The therapeutic relationship needs to be open to the child's projections. At times children can be dependent and see the therapist as an idealized self-object, as someone to look up to or be like. In Milena's early transference, the therapist mirrored Milena's grandiosity by allowing her to reverse roles and control the therapy, with Milena doing the questioning. By projecting her contemptuous feelings onto the therapist, Milena was also able to express her envy— her wish to devalue and destroy the therapist as a potential source of help and nurture.

Only much later on could Milena view the treatment relationship as a therapeutic alliance. Sandler defined this as "the child's conscious or unconscious wish to cooperate and accept the therapist's aid." Paradoxically, Milena achieved great milestones by going away to a non-English-speaking country for the summer and by getting into the college of her choice by operating totally on her own initiative. Since Milena needed to demonstrate and exercise her newfound capacity for autonomous functioning, she consulted the therapist only after being admitted to these programs. The therapist, as a "new object," needed to respect this newfound ability.

RESOLUTION OF AN IDEALIZING TRANSFERENCE

Case Example

By the third year of treatment, Maia (discussed in Chapter 2) had developed into a cheerful, pretty, highly intellectual girl. She became a leader in her therapy group at school, pushing others to work at the treatment process rather than employ resistance by discussing rock concerts, clothing, and so on. She had once been envious of those girls' experiences, which now seemed frivolous to her.

Maia was now preoccupied with an academic problem—her tendency to procrastinate when she had a paper to write. She discussed one paper that was illustrative, the social worker believed, of the transference at that point, which was almost totally idealizing. Maia had to write on the book *The Portrait of a Lady,* by Henry James. She described wishing to focus in particular on the relationship of Isabel Archer, the young heroine, to Pansy, a timid adolescent about to be sold by her parents into a powerful marriage. Maia felt that Pansy might admire Isabel, who was spirited, feisty, and independent. But she can't really be like her, Maia reasoned, nor should she be; those are fine qualities but they are not Pansy's qualities. Maia believed that Pansy nevertheless knew that Isabel would rescue her in the end. Maia and her therapist were able to discuss Pansy's relationship with Isabel in light of their own relationship and Maia's need now to be herself.

THE TRANSFORMATIONAL OBJECT

Christopher Bollas described the therapist as a "transformational object." He suggested that the mother of an infant must utilize her ego functions on behalf of the infant and that this would enable the infant to begin to use his own ego functions within the initially protective transitional space between mother and child. The therapists who treated Milena and Maia performed such a function. They bridged the transformation from symbiosis to autonomy for their clients.

CHAPTER 11

COUNTERTRANSFERENCE

TOLERATING REGRESSION

In a lecture to child analysts, Bruno Bettelheim once commented that there was only one requirement a child therapist needed to have: an ability to tolerate regression. He added that this ability is actually difficult to achieve and that many therapists are unable to acquire it.

Child therapists need to be able not only to tolerate the "regressive pull" of their child patients, but to be conscious of regression in themselves. At the same time, they must be differentiated enough to make use of regressive feelings as an empathic, therapeutic means (Ogden, 1982).

Countertransference with children is possibly more powerful than work with adults, because children can be regarded as fundamentally powerless in the world of adults. Child therapists can feel overwhelmed by the burden of acting *in loco parentis* when their clients are functioning without parental guidance. Nonetheless, every child therapist's countertransference will have its own particular characteristics, expressive of the therapist's unique personality.

RESCUE FANTASIES AND SPLITTING

Rescue fantasies are perhaps the most common form of counter-transference. Such fantasies can be helpful in that they enable thera-pists to work with very difficult, often impossible, situations. They represent certain pitfalls, however, to successful treatment.

Excessive identification with the child is of primary concern. This is actually a form of splitting. It is very easy to side with a child against parental figures and to regard parents as bad. This is espe-cially a hazard with cases involving loss or abandonment, neglect, trauma, and physical and sexual abuse. Sometimes there are very real reasons for this form of splitting, which has been called "objective countertransference" (Spotnitz, 1987). The therapist needs to toler-ate and understand this form of hatred (toward the child's parental figures), so as to modulate these feelings into useful therapeutic in-terventions both with the child and the caregivers. In residential treatment and other institutional settings, this form of splitting and hatred in the countertransference sometimes extends to other care-giving staff members. (This is particularly a hazard with child care staff, who are often the disciplinarians of children in residence.) The therapist's own childhood struggles become an issue in siding with the child patient. Often therapists engage in an unconscious battle with their own parents as well as with the parents of the patient.

The Manic Defense in the Countertransference

In the most extreme situations, such as foster care, residential treat-ment, and other situations where abandonment themes are pro-nounced, therapists may have fantasies of adopting a patient. Unfortunately, this is acted upon in institutional settings all too fre-quently and is a highly destructive form of acting out, both to the child and to the therapist. This fantasy needs to be worked through in supervision, as it is almost always disastrous when acted upon.

This form of acting out is a manic defense, an attempt to deal with loss by moving too quickly into action that is ultimately destructive. The manic defense is characterized by a triumvirate of responses to loss and psychological injury: triumph, control, and contempt. These responses are different defensive means of overcoming narcissistic injury; that is, one triumphs over the object, controls the object, and ultimately has contempt for the value of the object (Klein, 1935). This form of acting out is a grandiose fantasy on the part of therapists who believe they can magically resolve the child's tragedy by being a better parent to the child. The child's real parent is triumphed over and dismissed in the therapist's fantasy.

SPLITTING AND IDENTIFICATION WITH THE PARENTS

Another form of splitting is to dislike the child and side with the parents. Children can be off-putting because of their narcissism and dependency and because of their often uninhibited expressions of aggression and regression. Children who are excessively involved in autoerotic behavior or who are out of contact can also be experienced as obnoxious or rejecting of the therapist (especially by therapists who need to see themselves as nurturers). This can provoke early unmet infantile feelings in the therapist.

Therapists can become consciously or unconsciously resentful of children who are openly obnoxious or devaluing. This response is understandable, but it needs to be worked through in supervision by acknowledging—that is, "owning"—the feeling, however uncomfortable one may be to accept the fact that one feels contempt for a child. Often, such feelings can be relinquished when acknowledged fully.

Child therapists who are themselves parents also need to guard against identifying excessively with the child's caregivers. (This type of countertransference reaction is more subjective in nature.) A "subjective countertransference" involves elements of reality in the therapist's life. For example, a therapist who is also a parent may be thinking of their own fears as parents and address the child patient as if the child were in fact their own child.

Occasionally, therapists experience anxiety over the acting out of children. One unfortunate response to this is to set unrealistic limits or to impose excessive structure on the play therapy.

The most basic tenet of child psychotherapy is to follow the fantasy content of the child's productions. Some child therapists insist upon the child patient "playing a game strictly by the rules of that game"—(i.e., rules must be adhered to when playing board games, etc.). This form of rigidity is a mistake, because children who are lacking in internal structure simply cannot follow rules any more than a two-year-old can. On a certain level, the child patient may even find rules incomprehensible. Here, the child's fantasy must prevail for the sake of the therapy. Children who have been emotionally deprived (i.e., children who are developmentally at a preoedipal level), often act like younger children, because they have not developed enough ego strength and an age-appropriate superego.

Conversely, children who are more neurotic, who have begun to attain superego functions, cannot avoid playing by the rules. These children object when they are given an advantage in a game or when a game is made too easy for them to win.

Therapists who work in institutions often feel as responsible as parental figures when their child patients embarrass them by acting out, failing in school, and so on. It is as if the therapist assumes the role of parenting literally and feels shame for the child's pathology or for not having cured the patient. (The staff can collude with this fantasy by blaming the therapist or by holding the therapist responsible for the child's regressive behavior.)

HATE IN THE COUNTERTRANSFERENCE

Winnicott's paper "Hate in the Countertransference" (1947) is an examination of the experience of ambivalence and hatred on the part of the therapist as a response to treatment. During World War II, Winnicott and his wife took in a runaway nine-year-old boy who was in a youth hostel. (It should be noted here that citizens were encouraged by the British government to take in those made homeless by the war.) Out of this experience, Winnicott learned firsthand about hatred in the countertransference, as he and his wife struggled with a very abusive child.

Winnicott noted that therapists can feel hatred for their patients, just as parents can feel hatred for their children. Patients can be abusive, frustrating to help, and ungrateful for what they receive. Winnicott (1947) said that therapists must display "all the patience, tolerance and reliability of a mother devoted to her infant" and that they must "recognize the patient's wishes as needs." This is a great strain on the therapist. It is important for therapists to examine the anxiety (and hatred) that severely disturbed clients can produce in them. I discussed the problem of treating provocative children in Chapter 7.

IDEALIZING COUNTERTRANSFERENCE

Child therapists often view the child patient's special abilities or talents narcissistically. They overidentify with the child's intellectual gifts and unconsciously view the child as a part object (as does the stage parent). This idealizing countertransference is evidenced when a therapist boasts excessively of a patient's abilities.

It is also problematic when a child has an idealizing transference to the therapist. The therapist can feel gratified by this form of transference, which meets a deficit in the child and reflects the child's need for an idealized self-object. When the child is ready to relinquish idealization, the therapist must be able to recognize this turn in treatment and to enable the child to move on to other attachments. The therapist must watch for the very real hazards of viewing the child as a mirroring self-object.

Case Example (Mid-Phase Treatment)

When Maia began to heavily idealize her therapist, she described fantasies of identifying in specific ways with her. I have already described in Chapter 10 how Maia had a problem completing a paper for her English class. Recall that the paper was on a novel about a heroine and her relationship to a young girl. Maia had described the young girl as wanting to have qualities like the heroine, but Maia felt not only that the young girl was not like the heroine but that she shouldn't be like her. The therapist pointed out the similarities between Maia's need to be like her, the therapist, and the relationship between the heroine and the young girl in the novel. The therapist pointed out that while Maia might admire things about her, she still could and should be herself. This intervention allowed the patient to idealize the therapist if needed, but also allowed the patient to differentiate herself from her therapist—and ultimately from her family.

There are times when a therapist may have to act *in loco parentis,* especially when a child has inadequate parental guidance. This is commonly more an issue in outpatient child guidance work. In the next vignette, the therapist used her influence to help a young adolescent create a formal structure for her own safety.

Case Example

A twelve-year-old girl, Mary, recently released from residential treatment was doing reasonably well at home with her single mother. Although the child performed adequately at school and presented no behavioral difficulties, her mother did not set limits for her as to curfews. The child often found herself outside in the early evening long after her friends had gone home.

The child's mother worked and was easily overwhelmed and rarely available for child guidance sessions herself. The therapist felt that without adequate limits, the child would soon get involved with inappropriate activities. Since Mary looked up to her therapist, the therapist was able to assist Mary in creating structure for herself. The therapist worked with the child to set up appropriate limits, similar to those of her better-cared-for friends, including how much time to allot for homework and study, for watching television, for after-school activities, and so on. This intervention enabled the child to establish a structure for herself that was both internal and external and served needed self-protective functions.

THE FALSE SELF IN THE COUNTERTRANSFERENCE

Child clients frequently have long phases in the course of therapy that can feel boring to the therapist. At such times, the therapist might feel tempted to question the child excessively or might even feel pushed to interpret the play prematurely or too widely. Yet important integrative functions are often taking place during these periods. The therapist can easily feel distance and even alienated from the child during these treatment phases. This is notable when the therapist doesn't feel quite like her normal self. This exemplifies the false self in the countertransference.

Some children require silent mirroring from the therapist, especially if there has been excessive invasiveness of personal boundaries at home. (At those times children can be asked what they would like their therapist to do—i.e., talk or be quiet.)

Case Example

Mickey, then seven years old, spent a number of sessions studying a book of photographs from the movie *Superman*. He requested that his therapist remain silent during these sessions. Although his therapist complied with this request, she felt anxious, fearing that she was not doing her job sufficiently. The silence that Mickey required made the therapist feel useless (a false self state for a therapist to feel).

At a certain point, the child commented that he realized that Superman's father was married to a much younger woman, that he really was too old to have such a young wife. The therapist asked how old the wife should be, and Mickey responded that she should be more the age of Superman himself (as a man). In the next session, he asked his therapist her age and was astounded to find out that she was the age of his own mother. The therapist then began to notice that Mickey was suddenly behaving in a more age-appropriate style. He began to express more competitive feelings, replete with fantasies about besting the therapist's husband, his own father, and his peers. By dealing with oedipal material in the silent presence of his therapist, Mickey was then able to move on to play more aggressive, competitive, age-appropriate games with less anxiety than before.

SEVERE DEPRIVATION AND SECONDARY TRAUMA

Children in foster care, in residential treatment, and in hospices have often experienced multiple trauma, including physical abuse, life-threatening physical illness, and loss of important family members. The foster care system commonly has cases of children who have been moved several times, from one foster family to another. These children sometimes evince helplessness and resignation and frequently find new relationships not worth investing in. The therapist can be a target for aggression as a potential projected new danger.

As many families become decimated by drugs, jail—or today, by the AIDS epidemic—child therapists can experience a tremendous guilt and rage at their helplessness in the face of these all-too-common tragedies. Often, the staff in residences and institutions are buffeted by feelings of depression, frustration and helplessness in the face of systems that leave both children and their advocates helpless. Sometimes staff will develop psychosomatic or real illnesses, frequently miss work, and often feel frustration with each other in subgroups (e.g., therapists versus child care staff, etc.). Group regression in institutions is common when stressors are especially great. Subgroups may project persecutory fantasies and fantasies of anxiety over annihilation toward each other when stressors of the workplace are glossed over or denied.

Part III

MAJOR THEMES
in
CLINICAL SOCIAL WORK
with
CHILDREN
and
ADOLESCENTS

CHAPTER 12

PHYSICAL ILLNESS, DEATH, AND DYING

Anna Freud (1952) wrote of the effects of physical illness on the psyche of children. Writing from the perspective of ego psychology and drive theory, she highlighted the importance of understanding the psychosexual developmental phase of the child at the time of the illness. For example, a boy in the oedipal phase who undergoes surgery might be terrified of bodily injury because of his castration anxiety, and an adolescent affected by serious illness may experience deep distress over bodily image and issues of autonomy. Moreover, the parents of a seriously ill child are understandably terrified of losing their child and may become excessively protective and infantalizing.

D. Golden has suggested that psychological intervention "for children in hospital settings is an unqualified necessity" (Golden, in Schaefer and O'Connor, 1983). Physical illness in children may trigger regression; preoccupation with autonomy, mastery, and bodily damage; separation fears, especially if hospitalization is involved; fears of injury and death; and questions about an afterlife. It is important to remember that the body is as much a component of human identity as the psyche itself (E. Erikson, 1959). Self-representation—that is, the way we see and picture ourselves in fantasy—is affected not only by psychological but also by physical changes throughout the life cycle. Certainly, physical illness will be reflected in one's self-representation.

In working with children and adolescents affected by illness, it is important for therapists to note the underlying anxieties and their source, real or imagined. With physical illness, more than in any other type of therapeutic situation, it is paramount to acknowledge the reality of the client's experience first before exploring the client's fantasies.

Children's experience of pain and their conceptualization of physical disorder may be fraught with distorted perceptions. Panic and guilt are often aroused, and the magical thinking common to young children leads to feelings of being punished for bad thoughts or actions. In a sense, this is a form of grandiose thinking that is, understandably, used defensively as a means of feeling at least somewhat in control over catastrophic events. Denial is another mechanism used to avoid confronting terrifying thoughts.

Therapists occasionally collude with a child's attempts at denial. It is detrimental in the extreme for a therapist to use denial as a means of avoiding distress, even in the service of protecting a child. Parents, too, often utilize denial as a way of protecting the child (and, more often, themselves) from disappointment and despair.

It is very helpful to explain to hospitalized children and adolescents as much as is useful to them about what will happen. Children who can play out medical procedures can develop a means of coping and self-soothing. Group therapy is also a useful modality in physical illness. By sharing their preoccupations with each other, young patients can actively confront their anxieties and overcome a sense of social isolation (Golden, 1988).

CASE EXAMPLE

A twelve-year-old boy experienced exploratory surgery to investigate a middle ear problem that had led to loss of hearing. When he emerged from surgery, he knew that his hearing had not improved. His overanxious mother wished to tell him that his hearing had been corrected, in the hopes that the child would think so too. The social worker who met with the child told him the truth and said that further surgery in the future would be able to help his hearing. The child cynically replied, "I knew there was no difference. I knew I couldn't hear better." It was nonetheless a relief to him to have his own perceptions validated, to be reassured that he wasn't "going crazy."

In her autobiographical account of mental breakdown, *I Never Promised You a Rose Garden,* Joanne Greenberg describes experiencing abdominal surgery in childhood. The doctor tells her that they are going to fix her doll. The child knows that her doll isn't broken and that she herself is in enormous physical pain. In her later psychotic episodes, self-inflicted pain becomes a component, possibly because of the distortions experienced during this period of surgery. When her therapist, analyst Frieda Fromm-Reichmann, hears the story of this deception, she becomes angry on her patient's behalf. Her anger impresses the child, who silently renames her therapist "furii" (fury), thinking, "This one feels anger."

CASE EXAMPLE

Lindsey began psychotherapy at three and a half. She had been diagnosed at eighteen months with a form of muscular dystrophy. At the time of referral, Lindsey was having difficulty physically keeping up with her classmates, who were all physically challenged themselves. She was becoming increasingly angry and rejecting of her friends.

Children with a diagnosis of muscular dystrophy are typically at risk for premature death (often before age five) due to respiratory failure. Because of her condition, Lindsey had to sleep propped up and was at risk of developing serious illness even from a minor cold.

Lindsey used a walker and was learning to use a computer for writing and an electric wheelchair. Survival meant learning to cope with future difficulties, such as scoliosis and speech problems. Nonetheless, this was a child who tested in the intellectually gifted range. Like many children who are intellectually gifted, Lindsey was frequently overwhelmed by intellectual information that she could not adequately process emotionally because of her age.

Lindsey struggled with her increasing physical limitations. In one session, she wept over an encounter with a group of able-bodied children who urged her to run with them. She cried that she didn't want to grow up or get big. With her therapist, she played out this encounter with well-meaning but misguided children. Lindsey played that her therapist was a princess who rode in a carriage and that she herself was one of a group of normal children. She urged the therapist/princess to run and jump with her and her friends. The therapist answered that she couldn't do those things, that she rode because her legs weren't strong. Lindsey replied that they didn't want to be mean, that they just wanted to show her how to walk and run. The therapist/princess replied that she knew they meant well but that her feelings only got hurt when they urged her to do things she couldn't do. She went on to say that she was special but couldn't run and jump. Lindsey then said, speaking for the imaginary group of children, "We don't like her, do we? We like her carriage but not her." At this point, the therapist, stepping out of the play, looked into Lindsey's eyes and said, "I like the princess. I don't care if she rides instead of walks. She is very special, and I love her as she is." Lindsey was able to use this as a corrective experience. She later told family members that she was special and could be the way she wanted to be, not the way others told her to be.

In other sessions, Lindsey played at being doctor to a dying child. She wished to supply the mother with another baby. The therapist played the mother, who attested to her great love of her little girl, whose loss would be irreplaceable. These sessions show the therapist's ability to hear and address the concerns and fears of a three-year-old who faced the very real possibility of death. Sometimes in their play, the therapist voiced Lindsey's concerns and fears. At other times, she became the mother and voiced a mother's terror. Elisabeth Kübler-Ross noted that children who live with life-threatening illness usually know how serious their illness is and attempt to contend with the very real possibility of death, even when family members try to use denial. The saddest situations result when children feel that they have to protect beloved others from knowing the truth.

As her therapy sessions continued, Lindsey played at being dead many times. Often her play expressed a wish that her therapist be powerful enough to rescue her. In one session she played dead and asked the therapist to show her what to do. The therapist used puppets to try to rouse Lindsey, and the therapist had the puppets cry, "Oh, this is the saddest thing in the whole world!" Lindsey roused herself and scribbled on a blackboard, commenting that "when you die, people can mess up your stuff." Her therapist responded that "they can save it for memories."

As a result of her therapy, Lindsey could at least allow friendships to develop and could better contend with her anxieties of death and illness, knowing that they could be discussed with her family and therapist.

AN ADOLESCENT DIAGNOSED WITH AIDS

Tonio was an eighteen-year-old homeless Latino from the South Bronx. He was first diagnosed with AIDS by a mobile unit treatment team that routinely visited his neighborhood. The mobile unit was frequently the only source of medical treatment available to homeless adolescents. Many of the adolescents of this community who were diagnosed as HIV-positive had contracted HIV through sexual abuse from adults. The adolescents were wary of contact with hospitals and would only utilize the mobile treatment team that routinely came through the neighborhood.

Tonio's family agreed to treatment for him in a large community hospital. There he was able to make a connection to a social worker and described his future dreams. He wished to get an apartment of his own. He reported having been thrown out by his family after disclosing that he was HIV-positive and gay. He had lived subsequently on earnings from prostitution and frequently found shelter in crack dens.

After his hospitalization, Tonio was placed in an excellent hospice, where he could both live with other adolescents and have medical treatment. He was nonetheless determined to establish himself in an apartment ("to have a home of my own") and to live, like college students his age, a life emancipated from adults.

Concerned that he would otherwise return to the streets, his social work therapist urged Tonio to remain in the protective environment of the hospice. Tonio was adamant and did ultimately find an apartment. He became involved with a community church and had a quasi-familial relationship with a family active in the parish. He remained in contact with his therapist, as needed, up until his death. His church eulogized Tonio, celebrating his strength and giftedness in overcoming a traumatic life.

Tonio's social worker came to realize that it was in fact extremely important that Tonio realize his wish for autonomy and independence. Despite his wishes to protect Tonio and have him live safely, the social worker could see that it was important to respect Tonio's wish for some sense of mastery and normalcy.

In the past, many HIV-positive adolescents like Tonio expressed an unrealistic wish to start a family and lead a normal life.

Today, with current treatments offering hope for a longer life span, this kind of wish is not an impossible fantasy. As a result, it is now possible for HIV-positive adolescents to regard autonomy as a future goal rather than an immediate one.

Therapy with the terminally ill creates an inordinate amount of stress on the social worker. Today this has been termed secondary trauma. Like those who work in foster care, protective services, and residential treatment, these workers can develop the syndrome of burnout. The symptoms may include stress-related anxieties, psychosomatic illness, depression, chronic fatigue, and a sense of psychological numbness (Gabriel, 1996). Those who work with the terminally ill may find support groups helpful in processing the feelings of guilt, sorrow, and despair.

CHAPTER 13

SEXUALITY AND SEXUAL ORIENTATION

Therapists are often fearful of frank discussions of sexuality with adolescents. The reasons for this are understandable. They fear unwanted pregnancies; sexually transmitted diseases, especially AIDS; and the violence and abuse that sometimes accompany adolescent sex. The therapist's ultimate fear is being held responsible or liable for an adolescent patient's actions. When therapists cannot discuss sex with an adolescent client in language that is simple and understandable, they unwittingly communicate the idea that sex is somehow shameful and wrong.

Esman (1977) and many others have called for a reexamination of clinical assumptions and social theories about adolescence. Changes in society (especially as a result of the sexual revolution), an ever-advancing technology for contraception, the feminist movement, and the depathologizing of homosexuality—all have made many of the classical concepts of adolescent sexuality obsolete.

SEXUALITY IN FEMALE ADOLESCENTS

Altman (1995) considered how social class differences can result in projection. For example, aggression and sexuality can be disavowed by those of upper-class status and projected onto those who are less well off. This dynamic certainly applies to how sexuality in girls was viewed by society in the past (for any young American woman born after 1970, it is hard to imagine a time when abortion did not exist). Moreover, sexuality in adolescence (until relatively recently) was regarded essentially from a male perspective.

Tolman (1992) conceptualized sexuality from a female perspective by examining the social constructivist nature of sexuality in adolescents. She stated that girls have historically been seen as not wanting sex but, rather, as wanting intimacy and a relationship; sexual activity in girls was viewed as a means of getting a relationship. Tolman pointed to the dearth of psychological research on adolescent girls' sexual desire. She wrote that the "exclusion of the possibility that girls experience sexual feelings has obscured the need for psychological educative interventions" that might help girls to lead happier, safer lives.

Often the focal point for a study of female sexuality has centered on adolescents of color who are poor, a research tendency that limits the possibility of learning how adolescent girls in general experience desire. The question of sexual orientation in this group is rarely discussed at all.

The following case examples illustrate how social workers can discuss sexuality with adolescent girls.

Case Example

Claudia, a pretty sixteen-year-old Asian in group therapy, described the problem of achieving an orgasm with her boyfriend. She complained that her boyfriend always "wanted to be on top" when they had sex. She preferred to be on top herself, because she could bring herself to orgasm more easily that way. The other girls in the group looked confused and bewildered. The therapist asked if they understood what Claudia was talking about. She asked Claudia to explain what an orgasm was but finally had to assist in the explanation, as Claudia's definition was even more confusing to group members. The therapist described orgasm as the culmination of extreme excitement from sexual activity, a culmination, known also as a climax, that brings a sense of physical relief. The rest of the girls in the group discussed this idea very seriously. It had not occurred to them that sexuality might be a source of relief as well as excitement.

Claudia, who was more comfortable in using the technical language of sexuality, was at first pleased to talk to the others about achieving orgasm through masturbation as well as intercourse. She wanted, however, to then return to complaining about her boyfriend's selfishness. The therapist encouraged Claudia to be honest with her boyfriend about her preferences. She then returned to helping the other girls continue their discussion. The therapist explained to Claudia that she would be glad to talk further with her but that the group also needed help understanding sexuality.

Analysis

The therapist sought to address both Claudia's and the group's questions about sexuality. She did not view Claudia's presentation of her sexual problem as an opportunity to lecture the group on safe sex. She knew that Claudia and her boyfriend used condoms and that the group was aware of the need for safe sex. She felt that it was important for the girls to have their questions answered directly, without lectures on safety that could sound disapproving and moralistic about sexual behavior.

Case Example

Toni, a seventeen-year-old Greek girl who had recently lost her mother, had been in a relationship with a boy for two years. Toni and her boyfriend had recently graduated high school and were both about to leave for college. Although Toni was still mourning her mother's death, she described encouraging her boyfriend to have sex with her for the first time. She told the therapist about her experience of intercourse, saying that it was "nice" but that she thought it probably could be better, since this was her boyfriend's first experience of sex too.

The therapist congratulated Toni and said that she now knew what sexuality was like. She invited Toni to ask her any questions she had about sex or contraception, and the discussion proceeded.

Analysis

It would be easy to analyze this session in terms of Toni's loss of her mother and to regard her sexual activity with her boyfriend as somehow a reaction to that loss. At a later time, this might be appropriate for discussion, but in this instance the therapist was turned to as a mother, the kind of mother who can give her daughter permission to grow up and separate and engage in gratifying sexual experiences. It is rare that girls receive any encouragement or acknowledgment of their sexual desire; this has usually been reserved only for boys. Girls, like boys, enjoy sex because it feels good.

Many adolescents describe falling in love for the first time as a cataclysmic experience. For some, the breakup of the relationship is so overpowering that the deepest level of mourning is triggered. Often the lost relationship engenders low self-esteem in adolescents who are abandoned; they feel they are not attractive or will never be loved again. Occasionally, the mourning itself can be a displacement for the renunciation of oedipal attachment to a parental figure.

I have observed that adolescents with highly narcissistic or unavailable parents often enter into early inappropriate attachments in adolescence and are unable to renounce them. They often seek therapy for help in doing so.

Case Example

Julia requested therapy at age nineteen for help in terminating a relationship with her high school sweetheart.

As a thirteen-year-old, Julia had divided her time between her divorced parents. Her mother often left her alone during her high school years to visit a commune in the country. Julia's father, reportedly a self-involved, somewhat arrogant man, had remarried and often requested that Julia baby-sit for his new family, which included two young children.

Julia had met Joe at age thirteen and was especially taken with his mother, whom she described as kindhearted and mothering. Julia described Joe at age twenty as someone who was essentially lost. He worked sporadically as a carpenter and smoked pot every day. Julia had been fortunate in attending an excellent private day school, where she was regarded as a very gifted student. She had attached herself to several young female teachers at the school, whom she viewed as "bright and progressive" and saw as role models and mentors.

Julia believed that her need for therapy and a therapist was similar to her need for a special relationship with her teachers and with Joe's mother. The teachers and Joe's mother had once provided her with support and encouragement, and the therapist realized that she must perform a similar function in enabling Julia to move on to more gratifying relationships. The therapist also realized that she would play a transitional role with Julia, partly as a mothering figure, like Joe's mother, and partly as a mentor, like the progressive teachers who had taught Julia. She would also provide a bridge for Julia to early adulthood. Thus, the therapist found herself not only in an "old" transference figure relationship but also in a "new" relationship (Altman, 1992).

ISSUES OF SEXUALITY
AND ORIENTATION

Sixteen-year-old Rob applied for treatment himself. He believed he was gay and requested help in "making up my mind." He requested individual therapy, as he felt a deep sense of shame. He wished to resolve his sexual identity without parental influence; fortunately, his parents supported his request for therapy and were able to respect his privacy.

Rob described a fairly uneventful upbringing. His family was middle class, and his parents' marriage was intact. Both parents were essentially supportive of Rob, but the therapist noted from Rob's history telling that they seemed intrusive and prying at times.

Rob described always feeling a same-sex attraction. He remembered a childhood incident of being taunted by other boys as a sissy at the playground. Rob remembered being very careful after this not to give any overt preference or attachment to a boy.

Rob's therapist made a pact with him: she would not try to push him to be straight or gay, recognizing that he must decide this for himself. She did agree to help him clarify his feelings about his sexuality and supported his discussion of it. Rob had requested a woman therapist, because he thought a woman "could understand my attraction to men" and also because he wouldn't feel attracted to her.

Rob looked forward to his therapy sessions. He felt this to be the only time he could acknowledge his deepest feelings. After a year of treatment, it became increasingly clear to both Rob and his therapist that Rob was consistently seeing himself as gay. Together they found out about several organizations that existed for gay youth, but Rob was too fearful to visit.

Gay adolescents typically experience inordinate shame as part of the coming-out process. Statistically, gay adolescents are at risk for depression and suicidal ideation due to the societal pressures of homophobia and prejudice. Over one-third of all completed youth suicides are done by gay youth (Grossman, 1994). In a study of gay male adolescents, Hunter, Rosario, and Rotherham-Borus (1993) found that 68 percent reported substance abuse. Of these, 26 percent used alcohol on a weekly basis (Hunter, Shannon, Knox, and Martin, 1998).

In his sessions, Rob speculated on the possibilities of going to a gay bar or responding to newspaper ads in the personal section. The therapist shared with him her concern that by doing this he might expose himself to potential exploitation by adults or find himself in awkward situations from which it would be difficult to extricate himself. She encouraged him to consider a gay youth center as a place where he could meet and talk with peers and connect to a supportive gay community without fear of being humiliated or exploited. Rob needed a great deal of emotional support to be able to visit this youth center. Once he was finally able to do so, he befriended and talked to other gay teenagers in his own age group. This was an important intervention. After attending a number of meetings at the youth center, Rob decided to come out to his family. He was, happily, able to discuss his orientation and receive their support.

Rob returned to visit his therapist after a year away at a university. He described feeling annoyed at times at his therapist because she hadn't pushed him more in acknowledging his homosexuality. The therapist indicated that she understood how he could feel this way, but she reminded him that he had experienced his parents as excessively intrusive and pushy. If she had "pushed" him to acknowledge that he was gay, she would have been repeating the very behavior—threatening his autonomy—that he abhorred.

Although therapeutic intervention is a difficult process in cases of adolescent homosexuality, therapists can only assist their clients in resolving their sexual orientation and helping them find additional appropriate resources of support.

CHAPTER 14

FOSTER CARE

Therapeutic work with children in foster care may well be the greatest challenge for the most dedicated of clinicians. The lack of permanency and sometimes the uncertainty about whether or not a child can in fact be returned home add frustration to both child and therapist. Geershenson (1985) referred to the multiple foster care placements that sometimes occur as "serial separation trauma."

Separations can be wrenching and traumatic for both child and caregiver and are deleterious to a child's sense of permanency and object constancy. The sequelae of multiple placements are lack of trust, lack of belief in the future, and an inability to form intimate relationships.

When working with a child who has experienced a series of separations from caregivers, the therapist can helpfully construct a history for the child out of the narration of past events as a means of providing a sense of groundedness. This requires that the therapist work with the child in utilizing all the fragments of memory, including concrete details, that the child might offer. For example: "When you were three, you lived with the Joneses. That was where you told me you like the apple pie that Mrs. Jones made. When you were four, you lived with the Smith family in the trailer camp."

Although these remembered fragments, these tiny shreds of substance, sound pathetic, they nevertheless provide a framework for constructing a sense of order, however limited, out of the child's earlier life. It often helps children to have this history written down and to illustrate it with drawings, photographs, and montages of small objects from their past. These creations can be kept in the form of a scrapbook or journal. The process of constructing such a scrapbook is like making a model boat or airplane: it is a joint task shared between a child and an adult that is creative, nurturing for the child, and free of a requirement for a great degree of verbalization. (Verbalization is something that an adult in psychotherapy might do in reconstructing the past.) It should be remembered that memories, of course, are not necessarily accurate. Some memories, for example, combine several events into a single "screen memory."

The device of constructing a scrapbook of their past helps children to put words to feelings and thoughts and events. This clarifies and maintains a line of continuity and provides the groundwork for understanding cause and effect.

In psychotherapy yet another figure is introduced—the therapist, a being who is part reality and part fantasy to the child, an intermediary who clarifies the reality of the child's present and past and separates it from illusion.

CASE EXAMPLE

A child who had lived in eight different foster care homes before the age of three asked her therapist, "Remember when I lived in the trailer camp?" as if the therapist had been present throughout her life or had the power to magically delve into her past to know what she was talking about. The therapist reminded the child that she hadn't been in her life then and asked the child to tell her about it. It was more important that the therapist hear the essentials of the child's own story than to explore her reality testing or the accuracy of her memory. The therapist was being treated as an ongoing witness to the child's past life. In telling her own story, the child is able to bring the therapist into her world. The therapist becomes a witness to the narrative construct, to the child's life history as she experienced it. In this respect, the therapist is both a new figure to the child and also an old figure; that is, by way of the transference, the therapist enters into the child's fantasy about the past (Altman, 1995).

In the process of evaluating foster care situations it must be borne in mind that any change in the child's living arrangements will almost always bring about a degree of regression, even if the change is one that has been hoped for by the child.

CASE EXAMPLE

A seven-year-old girl had lived in foster care with a warm, nurturing family that had become quite attached to her. She was able to return home to her mother, whom she, in fact, had visited during her placement with her foster parents, who had arranged these visits without discussion with the caseworker. At the point that these visits began, the child became enuretic. The caseworker, who was inexperienced, thought that this warranted an automatic canceling of the plan for the child to return home. Her supervisor, however, understood that the appearance of the symptom of enuresis did not necessarily mean that parental rights should be terminated; rather, the caseworker needed to encourage the child to discuss her feelings and fears about leaving the safety of her foster family to return to her mother.

Analysis

This child's enuresis may have been a sign of anxiety about the difficulties she experienced with her mother, but it may also have been an indication of a conflict of loyalty to both families that the child was experiencing. In any case, more time needed to be given to the child to gradually digest this change and to the social worker to carefully assess the situation. It would have been significantly useful to have had conjoint family sessions with both families, with and without the child present, to discuss the change that was about to occur for all.

The best possible plan would allow the child to maintain relationships with both the foster family and her mother. This would enable her to feel comforted by both families' continued presence and support and less threatened by the loss of her living situation.

In foster care, all too often the child's needs are superfluous to the caregivers, agencies, and the judicial system. Careful planning, in conjunction with family treatment, would bring about the best possible outcome for the child. Family sessions ought to include both foster care and biological families, if at all possible. If the child senses that both families are working together with her or his best interests in mind and are not at odds with each other, then the common conflicts of loyalty to one family or another and the terrors over safety can be assuaged. Both families also deal with parallel fears. Open communication between the social worker and all participants in the placement process can help in moving the involved systems toward a less adversarial position.

Some families that are eager to adopt a child from the foster care system are well intentioned but naive in their expectation of a rapid adjustment (for either child or family). The problem most frequently encountered in adoption from the foster care system is one of denial. Foster parents often believe that a transition to family life is automatically easy, because the situation seems, on the surface, so much better than what the child experienced in the past. It can be quite a narcissistic injury to new adoptive parents to hear a child complain or accuse them unfairly. New adoptive parents of foster care children usually need a great deal of support from the therapist/social worker. The family may err in pushing the child to become one of them too soon.

CASE EXAMPLE

Rolando (discussed in Chapter 8), an engaging Latino child, was to be placed permanently with an American Caucasian family. The family lived on a farm with children of their own. They had spent many months visiting Rolando, and he had spent numerous weekends with them.

Rolando had been severely abused by his mother, who subsequently abandoned him and his sister, who had already been adopted by a family. Rolando had been placed in a residential treatment facility due to aggressive, impulsive behavior that made public school untenable. He was then to enter the foster care system.

Rolando, a handsome, winning boy with an Afro hairstyle, talked very favorably of his potential family but objected to their attempts at "Americanizing" him. For example, the family had given him a very American nickname, naming him after a little boy on a popular TV show about an American country family. The boy objected to this name to his therapist and pointedly commented that she pronounced his name appropriately (with Hispanic pronunciation).

The therapist had to address this issue gently with Rolando's adoptive parents. She pointed out that their understandable wish to take the boy quickly into their family had the result of making him feel threatened. Not only were they too quickly pulling him into the family orbit, without understanding that this needed time, but they were failing to understand the importance to him of his race and ethnicity (in fact, their deliberate change of name had the impact of making him feel that his Latino heritage and sense of self were bad).

CHAPTER 15

ADOPTION

Therapists who work with adopted children have long been aware of the intense conflict of loyalties that exist within these patients. This conflict is typically manifested by fantasies about the biological parents that are fraught with longing, loss, and mourning. Images of parents who are seen in fantasy as idealized, omnipotent, and occasionally tragic figures are heady antidotes to a more mundane, ordinary life. But there are other feelings that are hard to grapple with in treatment—feelings of abandonment. Such feelings can be described and labeled, but this ultimate act of abandonment is hard to work through (if that is possible).

Adoptive parents are commonly the recipients of displaced rage from their adopted children. As parents, they in turn must struggle with fears of being abandoned one day by their adopted child. Often, when a child presents enough difficulty to an adoptive parent, yet another abandonment can take place. One study found that an unusually high number of children placed in residential treatment had in fact been previously adopted. I have observed that when adoptive parents are open to their children's knowing about their biological parents and supportive of their curiosity, the children in turn are less conflicted (and sometimes less inclined to look for their biological parents).

In adolescence, adoptive children often struggle with identification with fantasied parents as well as with adoptive parents. Erikson

(1956) described the period of consolidation of ego identity in late adolescence as one of selective identifications and repudiations that become more conscious in nature, that is, more deliberate as a choice of a style of being.

THEMES OF IDENTITY IN ADOPTED CHILDREN

Case Example

Jimmy, an eight-year-old Asian boy, was adopted in infancy (at two months). He had been found abandoned at the door of a police station, a place where biological parents often abandon their infants. This was all the history that this child knew of his origins. Jimmy took some interest in his ethnicity, but at the period of time that treatment began he was unwilling to explore any further into the events or thoughts and fantasies surrounding his adoption.

Jimmy's adoptive parents were both Caucasian. Both parents were sensitive and caring, but they were undergoing a divorce. The divorce precipitated Jimmy's referral for treatment. He was described as impulsive and argumentative. He often played at being class clown and, as is typical of that role, was often provoked into acting out by other children. At home Jimmy argued endlessly with both parents but especially with his mother (who had requested the divorce). Although both parents were unusually patient, sensitive people, these arguments would often culminate in explosive temper outbursts on all sides.

Jimmy's adoptive father was an artist. Jimmy had learned drawing techniques from him and had already begun to develop a real gift for draftsmanship. In therapy sessions he often requested drawing material and asked that his therapist draw with him. He liked to appraise their drawings and commented on both his and her work in a matter-of-fact style, saying, for example, "That's nice; that's good." In a therapy session during a time when Jimmy was learning in school about the ancient Greeks, he drew the kind of columns that the Greeks designed—Doric, Ionic, and so on. He then drew a column that fit no model and drew a question mark underneath as if to say "What kind of column is this?" His therapist commented that it was "a Jimmy column." Jimmy laughed and looked startled at once. His therapist said that it was his column and no other.

Analysis

Children rarely speak directly about issues of adoption. This topic is simply too threatening to a fragile, developing sense of self. They do, however, speak to this subject in metaphor. Jimmy's affective response to his therapist's comment that his column was a "Jimmy column" reflects the accuracy of her interpretation of the question mark in his drawing (she deliberately chose to offer her interpretation within the metaphor of Jimmy's choosing). The therapist was metaphorically telling Jimmy that he is his own person, a unique individual with his own idiosyncrasies.

This therapist's comment left Jimmy free of the conflict of loyalty to either biological or adoptive parents. His column also reflected a deep question of his own identity. In terms of family and race, where did he fit in? Who was he? At times the therapist would comment that he was a gifted artist, like his father, acknowledging aspects of Jimmy's conscious identification with him, and that he had a love of reading and good verbal abilities, like his mother, thus recognizing his identifications with her.

Children in the latency period frequently idealize the same-sex parent or a same-sex teacher or other authority figure. In Jimmy's situation this was complicated by adoption and secondarily by divorce. His anger at his mother for precipitating the divorce also revived earlier feelings of abandonment by his biological mother. Jimmy's fears of the divorce were expressed as terror of what might happen to him if both parents abandoned him. The therapist brought this to his parents' attention in a family therapy session. Both parents then made it clear to Jimmy that he would never be abandoned by them (in fact, they not only held joint custody of Jimmy but intentionally lived near each other). In this session, Jimmy asked about what would happen if one of them died. They responded that in that event the surviving parent would live with him. They also described how his grandparents would assume custody if they were needed. By outlining in detail the chain of custodial relatives, they were able to give Jimmy a clear sense of protection and security in his extended family circle.

Their constant struggle to resolve issues of identity is a salient characteristic of adopted children. Jimmy's struggle with identity manifested itself in many ways during the treatment process.

In a later phase of treatment, Jimmy requested that his therapist read him the story *East of the Sun and West of the Moon*. In this story a little frog rescues a golden ball from a pond at the behest of a young girl. She has promised to grant three wishes to the frog but angrily spurns his requests—to drink from her cup, eat from her plate, and sleep in her bed. The frog is transformed briefly into a prince, who tells the girl that now, because of her selfishness, he must be banished to the land east of the sun and west of the moon. The girl, full of remorse, goes on a quest to find him. During her voyage she is told repeatedly that she "will find no welcome there." When the story ends happily with the reunion of the girl and the prince, the frog-prince can learn what his true nature is. This story was deeply compelling to Jimmy; he loved to add his voice to his therapist's when she read, "You will find no welcome there." For Jimmy, the story addressed the following questions: "Who am I? Will I ever truly belong to anyone? Will I be admitted to the fullest as a family member?" Jimmy's grief in his struggle to answer these questions, reactivated by his parents' divorce, made his struggle feel like a relentless and frustrating journey. Jimmy verbalized his hopes for the future: that one day he, like the frog-prince, would marry; that he would create a family; and that his children would look Asian, like him (an idea his therapist supported).

CHAPTER 16

MULTICULTURAL ISSUES

Social work has been the first of the mental health professions to acknowledge and respect the importance and impact of culture, race, social class, and, most recently, sexual orientation. It is a basic element of social work to have respect for cultural diversity. However, clinicians often avoid a discussion of cultural differences in an attempt to be tactful, somehow feeling that unless the client brings the subject up, it can't be addressed. This approach reflects an older style of psychoanalytic practice in which clinicians were taught to wait for the client to address a subject.

MULTICULTURAL ISSUES IN THE TREATMENT OF CHILDREN AND ADOLESCENTS

With children, as with adults, this failure to address cultural differences can often be a form of collusion between therapist and client. I believe that this collusion comes about because therapists fear somehow hurting clients by asking them about the stressors of difference. There also may be a great degree of guilt involved in not asking, that is, a sense of shame at not having suffered from racism or extreme poverty.

In work with children, difference is often addressed by the young client in disguised form, encoded in symbolic play or language. The therapist needs to be alerted to issues of race and culture that appear symbolically in the child's play.

Case Example

A white female therapist led a group composed of black and Latina latency age girls. The children loved to play out themes of family life. Frequently they assigned group members certain roles: mother, grandmother, daughters, and aunts. Occasionally, some (usually unwilling) girl had to play a boyfriend.

One particular drama involved the first date of one of the daughters. Preparations involved a great deal of dressing up and laughter from the girls. At one point, one child commented excitedly, "What a great group! We're all black here!" The group was enthusiastic in agreement, but one member shook her head and said, "No, we're not all black here." The other girls were puzzled and asked "Who isn't?" The child motioned to the therapist, saying, "She isn't. She's white." The group looked troubled and distressed. The therapist gently pointed out that that was so, that she was in fact white. She said that the group felt so much like a family that it might be easy to see all the members as family, all the same color. "Would you feel better understood if I were black?" she asked. The group could not discuss this further. They expressed a wish to return to their play, and in fact the play activity was quickly resumed. One child muttered that since the therapist was white, she must be a devil. The other group members tried to divert this child by a rush into frenzied activity, but the therapist responded to the comment by saying that she could see how someone might see her that way since she certainly looked different from the group. In addition, she was an adult, she said, not a child; that was different too. She wondered if the group could tell her more about themselves so that she would then understand them better; maybe then they wouldn't be afraid of her looking different. Although the girls seemed unable to continue this discussion at that point in their group's history, the subject of racial difference was at least acknowledged, preparing the way for further exchange at some other time.

Case Example

Marcus, a nine-year-old African American boy, interrupted his play to marvel at his white therapist's hair. He said, somewhat in puzzlement, "I bet a comb goes right through your hair." He then looked frightened, as if he had said something amiss. His therapist replied, "Yes, sometimes it does. Sometimes it gets tangled too, like anyone's. What is your hair like?" Marcus described learning to use an Afro pic, a wide-toothed comb, to fluff out his hair. He took out his comb to show her. The therapist admired the comb and said she knew that the teenagers often carried those combs too. Then she wondered aloud if he ever thought about his being black and her being white. Marcus held out his hand next to hers and pointed out that she wasn't exactly white and that he wasn't exactly black but more like brown. He told her that in his community, the therapist would be called "high yellow"—neither black nor white exactly, just lighter. He said he thought that was nice. The therapist said she thought he looked very nice too. She said she would be pleased if he would tell her more about all the colors of people and how his friends might describe them. Marcus was happy to do so; he said that he would tell her all about it and that it wasn't her fault that she was so ignorant. "That's all right," he said, "I'll teach you." She agreed and said it was true that she was ignorant and that he could help her learn something important.

Analysis

Boyd Franklin (1991) described how skin color and hair texture are ongoing themes of identity for African American women. He noted that skin color, in particular, is a source of shame; children of color are often excruciatingly aware of the variations of darkness and lightness as a result of racism. The Chinese child protagonist in the autobiographical novel *The Woman Warrior* relentlessly torments another Asian child for looking Asian and for not fighting back.

A West Indian woman told of her physical and sexual abuse in childhood. She said she was looked down upon by her family and neighbors because she was darker than the other children. She was, consequently, exploited by them.

Comments from a child client about skin color, facial features, and other manifestations of race and ethnicity can be used by the therapist to launch an exploration of self-esteem, self-identity, and the perceptions and teachings of the child's family of origin and community.

Case Example

Todd, a young adolescent African American, was referred to family court on a PINS (person in need of supervision) petition. He was referred because of excessive truancy. His father was additionally deeply concerned that Todd was exposing himself to neighborhood boys who were gang involved and much tougher. In the course of taking a careful history from Mr. Thompson, it was discovered that some years earlier Todd had been evaluated in his public school for learning difficulties. However, the results of the evaluation were never disclosed.

The social worker at the family court was well aware that the school system that Todd attended was indeed racist; for example, the system was too quick to transfer minority children to other schools without attempting to help resolve the sometimes minor problems. The worker investigated Todd's school history and found that he had, in fact, been diagnosed as dyslexic. This had never been addressed by remediation, nor had Mr. Thompson been told of his son's reading difficulty. As Todd advanced in school, he became understandably frustrated. Feeling more and more disconnected and humiliated in class, he began to truant and hang out with other boys.

The social worker met with Mr. Thompson and his son to disclose this information. He commented that it must have felt awful for Todd to sit through class and not be able to always follow the lessons. He also said that Todd's reading problem could be remedied with tutoring and extra help from school. The worker arranged for assistance for Todd from a sympathetic guidance counselor who promised to track his case more carefully.

The social worker, feeling deeply mortified by the callous system's disregard, apologized to Mr. Thompson. He commented that it might be additionally hard for Mr. Thompson to talk with a white social worker. Mr. Thompson graciously said that the worker had tried to help and had in fact succeeded. He said he felt that "black needed white and white needed black." Nonetheless, he said he had decided to put Todd into a private boarding school. His disgust with the system's neglect of his son convinced him that he had to act rapidly to protect him. The worker acknowledged that this made sense.

Before terminating treatment, Todd spontaneously one day brought a group of his friends to meet his social worker. They came in, somewhat awkwardly. The worker, thrown off guard, asked the group what they thought of their friend Todd and his difficulties. The boys offered various opinions—that school was boring, that Todd was a good guy, and so on. The worker agreed with this and asked if they had any suggestions. They didn't, but the worker realized that Todd wanted him to meet his friends, to enter his world, and to see that his friends were not the dangerous boys his father had implied that they were. By bringing his friends to meet his worker, Todd also enabled them to see another, more private and serious, side of him.

Analysis

The social worker in this case had to acknowledge to his clients the unfairness and implicit racism of the situation he had found them in. He was able to establish a greater sense of trust with his clients by conceding this reality than if he had attempted to gloss over the situation. Reality must always be reckoned with honesty.

MULTILINGUAL CHILDREN

In working with children who are multilingual, it is of primary importance for social workers to bear in mind the organizing function of language. This organizing function is reflected in cognition and affect. Words in one language do not always find an equivalent in another language. Affect can also shift in accordance with the language that is spoken. Language that is a person's primary, more familiar tongue may be associated with liveliness, warmth, and clarity of expression.

It has been suggested by Perez-Foster and others that the multilingual person's language choice can evoke powerful transference phenomena and can reflect resistance and repression as well as expression (Perez-Foster, Moscowitz, and Javier, 1996). Language also encodes symbolic material that is derived from important social interchange beginning in infancy with the family of origin.

Case Example

Six-year-old Mitzi, the only child of two émigrés—a Puerto Rican mother and a southern Italian father—evolved an ingenious linguistic means of contending with her complex cultural heritage.

Mitzi could pronounce words in Spanish and Italian with great accuracy as to the subtle differences in pronunciation. In her first session, she drew a picture of her family at her social worker's request. In her drawing was a house with a three-sided roof. On each side of the roof was a family member, and each was saying hello in a different language. The therapist could see in that first session that Mitzi was well aware of the different cultures and languages of her parents. Mitzi seemed to know all the different languages and pronunciations as well. She elaborated on these differences throughout the course of her treatment.

BILINGUAL ASSESSMENT

Analysis

Perez-Foster has argued for a psycholinguistic assessment of bilingual clients (Perez-Foster, Moskowitz, and Javier, 1996). She suggests exploring the age at which each language was acquired, the quality of the client's relationships with people who speak the language, any special psychodynamic or developmental issues surrounding the acquisition of the language, and the domain or usage of the language at present and in the client's history. The assessment should also include the language of dreaming and of internal thought.

In Mitzi's case, the three languages—English, Spanish, and Italian—represented different relationships, affects, and psychosexual phases. Spanish represented her mother and the fun and closeness of family. Italian represented a libidinally exciting father who was nonetheless distant. The two languages together also meant combat—a lack of agreement between parents. English became safe because it seemed less representative of conflict.

Mitzi's affect shifted with the language she used. Clearly, she felt closest to her mother's family. She described that family as being "more with it"—they knew how to dance and taught her to dance too. Her father's Italian family was associated with Sundays; symbolically, this meant elaborate family dinners, with all the members of a large extended family gathered around.

Mitzi was aware of her mother's contempt for her father's family.

This represented an additional problem for Mitzi, for it created in her a conflict of loyalties at a crucial developmental phase: six-year-old Mitzi was deeply enamored of her father, reflecting an oedipal phase residue. With great excitement, Mitzi related to her social worker that her father had told her that she was so pretty that she would probably be married by age sixteen. Her mother, who was currently struggling to complete advanced training in her profession, disapproved of this message to Mitzi. Like most children, Mitzi was well aware of those behaviors and attitudes her parents disapproved of; she would whisper to her social worker when she thought she was uttering something that would have made one of her parents unhappy with her.

In analyzing this client's situation, the social worker needed to be aware of linguistic cues that expressed the child's feelings symbolically. This included attentiveness to Mitzi's drawings that depicted various family scenarios as well as her playing out of family dramas.

These had to be understood from a developmental perspective as well. A six-year-old girl's positive oedipal attachment and preference for her father might add to her excessive provocation of her mother. Nonetheless, the social worker had to be attentive to Mitzi's wish to marry her parents to each other.

Part IV

THERAPEUTIC MODALITIES
and
SPECIAL PROGRAMS

CHAPTER 17

FAMILY TREATMENT

GENERAL ISSUES

Family treatment is one of the more difficult aspects of psychotherapeutic work with children. Most child therapists prefer working with children, because they can easily identify with them. The difficulty this presents to therapeutic work is that the therapist can easily side with a child against the parents, seeing the child as an innocent victim. If therapists are not in touch with issues of rage or conflict against their own parents, they will be prone to vilify the parents of their patients as a form of splitting. At the same time, it is important for therapists to recognize and acknowledge whatever injustices or abuses the parents of their child patients do, in reality, inflict upon their children.

A second difficult aspect of work with parents is that the therapist can also, sometimes understandably, side with parental figures against the child. This is especially easy to do if the therapist is a parent. Parents, in turn, are sometimes subjected to abuse (e.g., abusive language or provocative behavior) by their child. Again, therapists need to be conscious and aware of their own mixed feelings about their childhood and family of origin.

Therapists must be differentiated enough to view their clients dispassionately while still maintaining enough empathic connection to all participants in family therapy to continue to work therapeutically. To be able to follow the thought process of any individual, child or adult, also requires a degree of symbiosis to the client. Hence, a paradox is established for therapists: they must be able to be a recipient of communications from clients by being empathically attuned to language and conscious and unconscious processes while being separate enough to continue to function objectively and to analyze messages at all levels of consciousness (Ogden, 1982).

Obviously, family therapy is more complex for the therapist than individual therapy because many communications are being received at once. Additionally, parents in family therapy are often fearful of losing power and of being ridiculed in front of their children. Requiring special attention are clients who are recent émigrés, who are often deeply connected to their own culture's style of child rearing and at odds with the adopted country's dominant group.

In the early days of child treatment in social work, children were seen separately from parents, and parents were frequently assigned different individual therapists to avoid the conflicts described above. This approach created certain divisions: important information was often not relayed to parents about their child and serious information about parental behavior was sometimes not disclosed. If family work were not a part of child therapy, important family events, activities, or behavior patterns (e.g., physical, sexual, or emotional abuse or a traumatic event affecting all family members) could easily go unaddressed.

The early family therapists—Bateson, Jackson, and Haley of the Palo Alto group—pointed to the importance of addressing the family system's functioning. They described a family system as needing to maintain homeostasis, or balance. When one family member changes, the whole system is affected and will then strive to resume its balance by nullifying or countering the change. For example, if a scapegoated child receives therapy and is able to function well as a result, the rest of the family will redouble their efforts to maintain homeostasis and return to the old status quo. This underscores the deeply ingrained, resistant nature of behavior that is long established.

Typically, children with problems do reflect the difficulties of their parents. Sometimes a child's problems point to a problematic marriage or to depression in a parent, which may be acted upon in a variety of all-too-familiar abusive patterns.

One of the first tasks a child therapist must perform is to decide whether to utilize family therapy alone or family work in conjunction with individual child therapy. The correct approach for a given child patient can be determined in the first two or three sessions. If a family can utilize family work without continually scapegoating the identified child patient, then family work should continue. The therapist must, however, intervene quickly to stop any scapegoating of family members. If scapegoating persists or is intractable, it is advisable to separate parents from the child and to institute conjoint work.

Case Example

A family applied for treatment for their twelve-year-old daughter, Mary, who had been experiencing difficulties at home and at school. Since her parents' divorce, Mary's school performance had diminished considerably, and she had become argumentative at home. The therapist felt that Mary's difficulties were primarily reactive to her parents' volatile divorce and that in fact Mary's difficulty in functioning was relatively mild. In family scenarios, however, both parents continued to scapegoat Mary, as did both her younger siblings, even when Mary sat tearfully in the therapy session.

The therapist rapidly pointed out that if family members wanted to make use of treatment, they must stop blaming Mary for causing all the family's problems. The therapist commented that this was what they typically did at home and what they had come to treatment to try to change. She suggested seeing Mary separately at first, to hear Mary's side of the story, and then seeing her parents. This arrangement was suggested in order to establish a bond with Mary as well as her parents. When it became clear that the family was excessively interested in scapegoating Mary, the therapist decided to institute permanent individual sessions for Mary.

Intervention and Analysis

The therapist felt that Mary's parents wanted her to reprimand and scold Mary too. The therapist acknowledged to Mary's parents that this desire was understandable, given their frustration with her, but that therapy cannot be abusive if it is to be helpful. She commented that at a later time family work might be reinstituted. It was clear that the anger and contention that existed between the divorcing parents was being displaced onto Mary. This tactic enabled both parents to avoid the real pain and sadness the divorce evoked in them.

Not only scapegoating but also arguing and even violence can act as camouflage for sadness and depression in families. Mary's symptoms served to keep her parents united (in seeking and participating in therapy to relieve her symptoms) even as they blamed her. In individual work, Mary was eventually able to see that she was paying a high price in her attempts to keep her parents united.

WORK WITH A SINGLE PARENT

Single mothers and their children have come to represent the majority of the poor in America. Single mothers are often overwhelmed with the dual demands of parenting and financially supporting the family. It is difficult to balance these responsibilities while maintaining a personal life as well. One of the serious injustices of the psychoanalytic approach has been the propensity to hold the mother culpable for all the difficulties that children experience. Fathers have been excluded all too often from treatment—to the detriment of the family and also to themselves. When important family members are unintentionally excluded, they may begin to believe in their unimportance and act upon it.

Case Example

Mitzi, discussed in the preceding chapter, was the six-year-old child of a Latina mother and an Italian father. Mitzi and her mother were in frequent conflict. Dorrie blamed Mitzi for creating disruption in the family. Her mother had emigrated from Puerto Rico to America as a child; her father had left southern Italy as a young man. Mitzi's parents were never married. However, Mitzi's mother, Dorrie, came from a family where single parenting was acceptable, and Dorrie's family provided substantial support to mother and child. Mitzi's father, Paolo, also had a large extended family in America. He brought Mitzi to family gatherings on Sundays, which Mitzi looked forward to eagerly. Dorrie usually attended these gatherings as well. Mitzi was fortunate in being much loved and indulged by both extended families. When Dorrie began to express a wish to lessen her contacts with Paolo and his family, Mitzi became disruptive in school and at home. Dorrie expressed disgust with Paolo's lack of willingness to commit to marriage with her and became critical of his overindulgence of their daughter.

Mitzi, however, was deeply committed to bringing her parents together, a goal she expressed tearfully in one particular session.

Case Example

Dorrie was enraged at Mitzi to such a degree that the therapist thought it advisable to interview them separately, dividing the session equally. With Mitzi sitting silently, Dorrie described her rage at her daughter for being a constant disruption at home, especially while she was on the telephone with Paolo, as had occurred the night before this particular session. During that phone call, Mitzi became such a nuisance that her mother hit her and yelled at her. In her half of the therapy session, Dorrie expressed the anger she still felt toward her daughter. Mitzi then had her turn to speak. The therapist commented that she heard that Mitzi and her mother had had quite a fight. The therapist decided to utilize a paradoxical technique known as reframing. She acknowledged that Mitzi had done "a really good job" of turning the house upside down and distracting her mother. How had she done this? wondered the therapist aloud. Mitzi began to explain enthusiastically: "Mommy was yelling at Daddy on the phone, so I began pulling everything out of the cupboards."

THERAPIST:	Oh! Then what happened?
MITZI:	I pulled all the books and toys out and left them on the floor!
THERAPIST:	(*Still impressed*) Wow! Then what happened?
MITZI:	Mom continued to yell at Daddy and at me too. Then, I got on the sofa WITH MY SHOES ON!
THERAPIST:	(*Incredulous*) With your shoes on?
MITZI:	Yes. I began to turn cartwheels with my shoes on.
THERAPIST:	Then what happened?
MITZI:	Mommy got off the phone and hit me.

The therapist told Mitzi that she seemed to have done a great job of upsetting her mother. Then she asked the little girl what she thought might have happened if Mommy could have continued her conversation with Daddy. Mitzi suddenly became tearful. She said that Mommy had just called Daddy "a big J" ("A big jerk," she whispered). She was fearful that if the conversation continued, Daddy might become so angry that he would hang up and that she might never see him again.

The therapist then commented empathetically to Mitzi that she had done an excellent job so far of trying to keep her parents from fighting but that, as she could see, her plans didn't always work. The therapist went on to say that Mitzi was paying too high a price for keeping her parents' attention focused on her mischief and that they needed to work out their problems as adults. Mitzi's mother began to interrupt with another tirade, but the therapist asked her if she could see what Mitzi was afraid of—that she feared losing her father forever. Both Dorrie and Mitzi were in tears at this point. The therapist, attempting to keep her back to source, told Dorrie that she thought Mitzi needed to be reassured that even though her parents hadn't married, they would never abandon her. To Mitzi the therapist explained that she couldn't force her parents to get along or marry, even though she wished for this badly.

Analysis

By using a reframing technique, the therapist turned Mitzi's acting out from a symptom into a behavior that had a purpose. One way of examining repetitive behavior is to ask what purpose it serves. The repetition itself implies that the behavior has a very important function to the individual. In this case, the child's misbehavior was important to the homeostasis of this single-parent family. By providing her mother with the means of scapegoating her, Mitzi could keep her parents enjoined in interaction, even though the price she paid was excessively high.

Case Example

Mara was a thirty-year-old mother of two who was recently separated from her husband. She was raised by a caregiver in the West Indies who she believed was her mother; at age ten she suddenly learned that her mother was, in fact, in America. Mara described a childhood of extreme poverty. As the darkest of a group of children, she was often reviled and teased. She reportedly was used for all the menial tasks and was the first to be called on to run errands. Despite this, she felt loved by her caregiver, whom she called Auntie later on in life. As a child Mara had been sexually abused by a neighbor, who paid her back by giving her food and sweets, commodities that were in short supply in her family. Mara admitted seeking the neighbor out when she was hungry and said that at that time she felt affection for him.

As a young woman, Mara became strikingly beautiful. She arrived in the United States at age thirteen. From then on, her life was very restricted. Her biological mother was a cold woman who was excessively strict with her. Mara understood that this might be warranted, since she was growing up in the inner city; however, she was also kept from normal school activities.

Mara described her own daughter, age ten, as being a problem to her. The child was often clinging and demanding and appeared to favor her father. Mara had left her husband after a series of affairs with well-to-do white men. She discovered that her husband had a long-standing gambling problem and had squandered their savings. Mara had not allowed herself to recognize this problem for some time. She had, however, begun to recognize her anger at her dark-skinned daughter as being irrational.

With little assistance, Mara could connect her own feelings of being damaged, unattractive, and unwanted with her feelings toward her daughter (whose conception had forced Mara into marriage). In addition, Mara's daughter (who was loved by her father) developed a weight problem. In her daughter, Mara saw the childhood she had come to abhor.

As Mara made the connection between her feelings toward herself and her projections toward her daughter, she became more giving toward her child. She was able to stop other family members from teasing and criticizing her daughter and expressed pleasure in her daughter's boasting about how pretty her mother was.

This case was, in a sense, primarily reparative work with a parent and secondarily therapy for her child. If the child's symptoms had increased, the therapist would have asked to see the family and in fact had originally suggested this. Both Mara and the therapist agreed that this might be possible if the situation escalated, but given time and financial constraints, decided to wait. Mara was able to develop empathy with her daughter and was able to become a nurturing parent. Her daughter's behavior improved as a result.

CHAPTER 18

RESIDENTIAL TREATMENT AND DAY TREATMENT

Residential treatment facilities are schools for children and adolescents who cannot be maintained at home or in their community. Typically, the children and adolescents accepted for residential treatment have become dangerous to themselves and/or to others. They require a higher degree of supervision than a private home or foster care arrangement can provide.

In some instances children can live at home but need the therapeutic services of a day program. Day programs typically offer a specialized school with small classes; psychotherapy, both for the individual and the family; and recreational programs designed for the wide array of behavioral disorders evinced in this population.

At one end of the spectrum are children who are psychotic, bizarre, and, as a rule, extremely fragile. They are quick to decompensate and are, unfortunately, often a target for scapegoating by other children in the community at large. They often appear helpless and at a loss for appropriate responses. This group needs a structured, protective, nurturing atmosphere where repressive behavior can be tolerated.

At the other end of the spectrum of residential treatment populations are children who are extremely impulse disordered. They are often aggressive, violent, and destructive to self and to others. They too need a strongly supportive atmosphere that is highly structured; it must provide limit setting without being abusive and must emphasize the importance of reality testing, judgment, and the consequences of one's actions.

WORK WITH CHILDREN WITH PERVASIVE DEVELOPMENTAL DISORDER

Psychotic children represent the greatest challenge to child therapists. Here, the therapist must constantly decode psychotic language—i.e., language dominated by primary process. Primary process thinking disregards logical connections and confuses wishes and thoughts with reality. This type of thinking utilizes no sense of time—past, present and future are confused. Latency-age children (six to twelve) typically move into logical, grammatical reality-oriented thinking, called secondary process (Goldstein, 1995). The therapist must make sense of confusing dialogues that are often monologues, and yet respond in a supportive way to bolster ego functioning and reality testing. The therapist must find a balance between, on the one hand, supporting reality testing and helping to enhance the ego functions and, on the other hand, hearing and responding to the deepest level of primitive anxieties.

New therapists to this population need to learn patience both with the children and with themselves, given the difficulty of this work.

Case Example

The official diagnosis for Jason, a large, overweight African American twelve-year-old, was Pervasive Developmental Disorder. Jason was a child who was easily confused, displaying disordered thinking and extreme fragility. He was often scapegoated by the more aggressive children in his residence and under this strain would begin shouting nonsense.

Jason was extremely bright. However, he spoke in a code language. Not only his therapist but also the school and child care staff of his residence quickly learned this language. Jason's language used initials and the wording on signs (e.g., traffic signs) found in everyday life. This brand of language became a kind of linguistic shorthand for Jason, a way of distancing himself from feelings or frightening experiences.

Intervention and Analysis

In one session the therapist, knowing that Jason had been home over the weekend, asked him how his visit went. Jason replied, "H.B. [his name for his therapist], you take no parking at any time, you take yield the right of way." Jason's therapist knew that H.B. stood for *Human Behavior*, the title of a book in the therapist's office. Jason had previously appropriated this title for his therapist. "You take no parking at any time" meant that by asking about something personal, a home visit, the therapist was venturing into emotionally dangerous territory. "Yield the right of way" meant that the therapist should let Jason direct the conversation in therapy.

The therapist continued: "You don't want to talk about your visit? Was it hard?"

Jason replied (now laughing raucously), "H.B., you take stop, you take restricted parking, you take do not enter." Clearly, the therapist's innocuous question was overwhelming for Jason.

The therapist was correct in asking about Jason's weekend. Not to do so would have been irresponsible and would have had the effect of colluding with family members if a problem had arisen during Jason's visit and the family failed to report it. However, Jason's fragility was so profound that even an innocent expression of concern or curiosity from his therapist carried the risk of being interpreted by him as an assault. In this particular session, continuing with this line of questioning would have affected Jason's fragile capacity for self-cohesion, resulting in fragmentation, which in Jason took the form of irrational ranting and raving. The therapist would have had better success by meeting for additional sessions with both Jason's guardian and Jason—unless Jason refused or became distressed by such sessions.

Ordinarily, family work should not replace individual treatment; the exception is when the child is as fragile and disorganized as Jason. With psychotic children, as with psychotic adults, family therapy should be calm and structured. Highly intense, dramatic, histrionic family members can easily promote fragmentation in an individual with profound ego deficits. A personality structure this brittle collapses readily under such duress.

Jason preferred individual sessions and liked to sit at the piano. Although he showed no interest in learning to play the instrument, he maintained a real interest in learning to read music and in identifying the keys. Jason had perfect pitch—that is, he could sing any note exactly on pitch without assistance. He worked especially well with the residence's music therapist; he could engage somewhat in conversation with her while playing at the piano.

In residential work with children like Jason, it is important to allow them to develop a relationship with any staff member they select, since interpersonal relations are so difficult for them to establish. In a good residence, staff will also try to encourage in patients any nascent talent or ability as much as possible. Offering them a chance to cultivate an interest in music, art, sports, and so on, is important as a means of developing self-esteem and enhancing ego functioning and innate talents. Sublimation is regarded as one of the most important defenses utilized by higher-functioning individuals. Offering children and adolescents in residential treatment a chance to develop their skills and talents not only assists in strengthening the role of sublimation in their lives but also provides them with a new array of abilities to use in developing social relationships.

Case Example

Brandon, an African American eight-year-old, was admitted to the residence because of aggressive behavior at home and at school. He periodically lashed out at other children with little or no provocation. Additionally, he began truanting and running away from home.

Brandon had one older brother, who had lost contact with the family, a younger sister who was still in infancy, and a single mother, who appeared to love her son but was seriously depressed. Although family treatment was offered, his mother, who worked as a prostitute, rarely appeared for sessions. When Brandon's social worker attempted home visits, Brandon's mother was often not at home. The worker found it very helpful to involve interested child care staff in the home visits. In this way, child care staff could also have a glimpse of Brandon's home life and his therapy.

Once Brandon was admitted to the residence, he became increasingly frustrated by his mother's inactivity and lack of involvement in his life. He blamed his social worker for this. He claimed that she was the most powerful and important person at the residence. He believed that she could "make" his mother "behave" if she chose to but that she was "lazy, selfish, and didn't care about anybody but herself." The worker attempted to reason with Brandon but failed to help him see the unspeakable—that his mother, in effect, was abandoning him.

As Brandon's mother began to disappear for longer lengths of time, the protective service agency involved in Brandon's case decided to terminate her parental rights. At this point, Brandon began to regress more seriously; he hit staff members and had to be restrained. He sometimes had to be terminated midway through his therapy sessions owing to the severity of his decompensation. He would, for example, climb under a table in his therapist's office, spitting and cursing at her. He became increasingly disorganized in his thinking and was found to be collecting and saving his own feces (this is not an uncommon phenomenon with children who are extremely regressed).

Brandon's therapist acknowledged his anger at her and said that it was understandable that he would feel this way and also that it was all right. She said that she wanted to make him feel safe and that he would remain at the residence for as long as he needed. She told him that his mother did love him but that right now she couldn't be relied upon to visit him. She promised to keep on trying to help his mother and said that maybe, in the future, his mother would be able to use that help.

It was important here to allow Brandon to express his overwhelming despair and rage. Witnessing the depth of an abandoned child's grief is one of the hardest feelings for child therapists to tolerate. Abandonment is incomprehensible to a child. Bowlby characterized the response of infants to abandonment as being first an expression of protest and then one of despair and depression. Depression has the quality of defeat (Bowlby, 1998).

Brandon and his social worker had to sit through his loss. Some experiences can't continually be analyzed; rather, they must be lived through.

After the court hearing, however, an interesting turn in Brandon's treatment took place. The social worker told Brandon that the court had decided to give parental supervision rights to the residence and that his mother had not contested this. Brandon's behavior changed abruptly. He began to talk coherently to his social worker. He characterized the court hearing, which he had not attended, as being the day his mother gave him away. (His mother had not appeared for the hearing.) Brandon began to unpack his belongings (up until that time, he had threatened to run away and had kept his things in a knapsack) and to put pictures on the wall of his bedroom. Impressively, he became deeply involved in learning, both in the agency school and with his social worker.

As Brandon began to recover from abandonment depression, he began to value very small things. Presents for his birthday and on Christmas, for example, became highly important to him; he would carefully remove the wrapping paper and ribbons and save them, giving them equal importance with the actual gift. Significantly, he put these on his walls as well. At this time, Brandon began to play a certain game with his therapist: he would ask her to tie the gift ribbon and bow around his waist and attach it to herself. By tying himself to his therapist, Brandon emphasized the attachment he had to his social worker and his total dependence on her now that he had lost his mother. However, this behavior was a displacement of his attachment to his mother; it was as if he thought that by being tied to his therapist he might never have lost his mother.

The therapist enacted this play with Brandon with minimal commentary at first. Only over time, as he became emotionally stronger, did she attempt to comment. At first she said only that he seemed to like to tie both of them together, that now they could go everywhere together and that they would never lose each other. Sometimes hyperbole is useful with children: "Wow! We'll be tied together forever now. What do you think that will be like?" The use of hyperbole, with its dramatic emphasis, expresses the wish in the child's fantasy.

Gradually, Brandon began to talk more in his treatment sessions; he continued to use metaphorical language to address the themes of family, closeness, and attachment.

Although Brandon's therapist was assigned to working with the boys unit of the residence, she continued to work with girls from the girls' unit. Brandon objected to this and jokingly informed his therapist that she should not be seeing girls anymore; he insisted that she was a boys' therapist and that that position was better. His therapist joked with him and said that she really liked her work with the boys but that she liked the girls too—after all, she herself was a girl. Brandon replied that she wasn't a girl, she was a therapist and that she should behave like an important therapist of the boys' unit.

Clearly, Brandon had now moved into a period of greater ego stability. He was able to joke and to tell his therapist his concerns and his annoyance at her. By questioning her loyalty to the boys' unit, Brandon saw her as an unfaithful or unreliable mother to boys—not behaving as a mother ought to.

It is important to recognize that as therapy progressed, Brandon was able to utilize more symbolic thinking. Melanie Klein (1930) wrote about the transition from instincts and concrete thinking to more abstract thought via the use of symbols and symbolic metaphors. In Brandon's case, the boys' unit was a metaphor for family and also as a symbol of loyalty. By joking with his therapist, he was able to carry on a dialogue with her that expressed his feelings and indicated his greater ego stability. He felt safe enough to tease her about his annoyance and disappointment in her, instead of spitting and hitting her.

In residential treatment, social work therapists must be extremely flexible. Often the therapist will need to develop alternatives to working in the therapy office and adhering strictly to the scheduled length of the session. Therapists in this community must be as responsive as possible and must have an enhanced capacity to tolerate frustration.

When residential treatment therapists participate in group activities with their child patients, they often learn about a child's latent interests and abilities. For example, Brandon's therapist discovered some unique qualities and talents in him during the course of a school trip to the zoo, where Brandon displayed great interest in learning about the animals. His therapist asked him if he would like her to read the commentary posted near the exhibit of each animal species. He acquiesced readily and listened attentively to the information. His therapist later commented on this to the general staff meeting of the boys' unit. When Brandon's eager interest in learning was corroborated by the residence's teaching faculty, the residence team decided to encourage his learning as much as possible by giving him books of his own, and extra attention in learning and utilizing independent study. The staff were deeply gratified by Brandon's move forward.

Analysis

Initially, Brandon appeared frail and impulse disordered. Under the duress of the court hearing at which parental supervision rights were transferred from his mother to a residential treatment center, he began to decompensate. With children and adolescents like Brandon, it is useless to demand the kind of behavior that one expects from a healthy child. Rather, the therapist must be flexible enough to help the child begin to create internal structure. This is akin to helping a toddler slowly learn to play by the rules. In the next case, this was very much in evidence.

CHAPTER 19

GROUP TREATMENT
WITH CHILDREN

Group therapy with latency age children, like individual therapy with the clients of this age, is activity based. Typically, children between the ages of seven to twelve do not talk continuously in therapy; rather, they intersperse discussion with activity. Often the activity is focused around a project (e.g., a creative art enterprise) or around games. Sometimes a game is chosen over and over again and represents an important theme in the child's life.

Group treatment replicates the family of origin in several respects: the group re-creates the psychodynamics of family life, members do not choose which group they will join, and members exist in an interpersonal world born out of dependency on each other.

Traditionally, latency age groups were circumscribed by age and gender. Recently, some groups, notable in public school settings, have been composed of members who share a common theme or issue, for example, recent immigration, divorcing parents, or bereavement.

Optimally, each child should be interviewed before being placed in a group therapy situation. Children who are too physically aggressive or abusive of others may not do well in group therapy and are frequent targets for scapegoating by other children. The experience of witnessing a child being scapegoated by other group members may be frightening to some children, and group attrition may be the end result. In interviewing potential group candidates, it is useful for the therapist to ask them questions about their expectations. The interview should take place in an individual therapy setting. As part of an introduction to the group experience, the therapist should explain to children that group is a way of being with children their own age and that it is a chance to help other children with their problems and to be helped by them in turn.

Here are some questions for the therapist to ask a potential group member:

1. If you seem very quiet in group, would you like me to ask you about this or would you rather speak when you are ready? (This question attempts to clarify the extent to which the child will ask and allow for help from the therapist-leader and the extent to which the latter will allow for more autonomous stirrings in the child.)
2. If another child says or does something that bothers you, how would you like to handle this? Would you like me to intervene? If not, how might you resolve a conflict? (If the child's answer includes hitting the offending child, ask that the child try not to do this and try instead to put feelings into words or ask the therapist for help.)
3. How would you feel about being in a group with children who may feel differently about things than you do?

These questions serve two purposes: first, to see if the child can be flexible in behavior and use the therapist for assistance rather than acting out; second, to assist the therapist in determining if group treatment is an appropriate modality for the child under consideration.

The questions help each potential member realize that fellow group members will be different from one another, that group treatment is, fundamentally, a way of negotiating those differences and also of recognizing the different feelings people have, and that group treatment is a form of learning to work cooperatively.

GROUP EXAMPLES

A Latency Age Girls' Group

The Social Club, so-called by its members, was composed of eight girls between the ages of eight and eleven. The group was mixed ethnically and racially. The girls came from middle-class families and had not been deprived in financial or social terms. Seven of the eight members had lived all or most of their lives alone with their mothers. Six members were the only child in the family, and only one member came from an intact nuclear family and had a sibling. Group meetings were conducted at a locally well-known neighborhood community center. Five girls were Jewish, one was a white Anglo-Saxon Catholic, and two were of mixed racial identity. Of particular importance in these girls' background is the fact that all of their mothers worked out of necessity. The girls initially came to the center's afterschool program in lieu of other child care arrangements.

The majority of members in this group suffered from varying degrees of depression. In addition, two were socially withdrawn, one was obese, and two had interpersonal difficulties and were considered to be acting out children.

In this country, the intact nuclear family has undergone a steady erosion in the last fifty years. Single-parent families have increased not only as a result of divorce and widowhood but also because increasing numbers of women have opted to become single parents by choice. Living in a family headed by a single parent demands new coping mechanisms for children's adjustment. The new family structure not only affects a child's psychic defense strategy but has implications regarding identity formation.

Girls who watch their mothers coping alone have begun to adjust to the single-parent family. In families where a father's presence is unknown in the household, girls struggle to combine the qualities of traditional femininity with the need to protect oneself (i.e., instead of relying on a father for protection). Girls of such families may fantasize less about the male–female dyadic romance and attempt to incorporate male and female selves.

The thematic material of the Club began to emerge in the very first session: the need for an idealized self-object transference expressed itself in the persona of the superheroines.

American popular culture has had a predilection for providing superheroes as sources of identification for latency age boys. The very concept of childhood itself has been described as a culturally derived invention. As such, it follows that expectations of a normative latency must change (or adapt) as the culture itself changes and adapts over time to changes in the structure of family life. In Maxine Hong Kingston's book *Woman Warrior,* the adolescent heroine periodically retreats to fantasies of empowerment involving a woman warrior.

S. R. Slavson was one of the first therapists to conduct activity group therapy with children (Bucholz and Mishne, 1994). In recent years, there has been an emergence of superheroines for girls: Supergirl, Wonder Woman (who dates to the mid-1940s), and an assortment of pretty policewomen. The Social Club (the name reflecting the Slavson tradition of children's groups) early on periodically referred to the adventures of a family of superheroines on television and in comic books. The leader of this fantasized group led the Rebellion, which was against a group of men who were authoritarian, militaristic, old, and cruel. The men were the ruthless rulers of the kingdom, and they frequently employed robots to carry out their warfare against the Rebellion. In a sense, they represented a mechanistic antinature force. (Janine Chasseguet-Smirgel has suggested that men often treat themselves as machines and that dehumanization is more popular among men than creativity.) In the girls' fantasy, women represented the force of creativity that conquers all.

The girls' fantasy of the Rebellion is akin to a secret society whose leaders serve as the ego ideal. Hence, group members shared an identity in belonging to the Rebellion and shared group ideals.

In the first sessions of the group, one member brought her Peeka-Blue doll. When the group leader asked her what kind of doll it was, all the group members came over to tell her that the doll was a member of the fantasized leader's family. It is of significance that this doll character was known as "the watcher" and guardian, functions that can easily be associated with the therapist's role. The doll served the function of transitional object. In this case, the "watcher" watched over the child herself as a protective force. The group had already collectively begun to point toward the emergence of transference component requirements.

The early group meetings centered on the girls' playing and discussing plans to adorn themselves. They liked to make jewelry and would often engage in trading spangles and jewelry beads with one another. They discussed various fantasies that hinged on the future: how they planned to dress as adults, especially as very fancy women, and their wishes to be like famous female performers (rock stars and models). One girl described a plan she and her best friend had: they were going to perform on the sidewalks until they had enough money to dress like Madonna and go on the road to Hollywood.

Loewald (1974) discussed the need to envision a future for the ego: "The ego ideal represents a return to an original state of perfection of the ego not to be reached in the future but fantasized in the present . . . it becomes an ideal for the ego seen in a much more differentiated and elaborated form than previously in parental figures. . . . Here the future is envisaged for the ego, but not yet a future of the ego."

Conflict within the group initially nearly always was diverted by means of a return to jewelry making, an activity the girls would turn to throughout the group's existence. Interpersonal conflicts appeared to be temporarily resolved by a preoccupation with adornment. During these periods, the jewelry making and trading of beads were done in a very serious, intense manner. The group leader speculated that conflicted feelings in the lives of these girls were usually handled by avoidance. Conflict in the group was dealt with by members by attempts to be very cooperative with one another—and, in the beginning, with the group leader as well—in an effort to preserve the group as a family. The return to narcissistic concerns (jewelry making, adornment) might have been the safest route for girls whose family life lacked siblings and a second parental figure and who therefore had a need to enhance themselves.

A classic view of this preoccupation with jewelry (i.e., the family jewels) and adornment would be to regard the jewels as male genitalia. Seen in this light, the girls had neither male genitalia nor fathers. A preoccupation with self-adornment is a means of restoring self-esteem in the face of deprivation. These girls were deprived of their most significant heterosexual relationship (the father); they suffered, consequently, the loss of an archaic grandiose self-object—the admiring father who can reflect back the little girl's grandiose strivings for admiration and, ultimately, romantic love.

The group often gathered around the worktable to concentrate on games or jewelry making. At these times, one or two girls might request help with a game or involve the group leader in a discussion. While the group leader gave her attention to these girls, another girl would frequently sidle up behind her and begin to braid her hair, making suggestions as to how she, the group leader, might wear it. One child, Melissa, suggested that the group leader would definitely look like a teenager if she shaved her hair into a Mohawk and dyed it purple (the group thought this was a fine idea). At these moments the group leader became to the girls more of a sister group member and hence shared in the adornment preoccupation.

The group enjoyed a dreidel game, which members set up to be played by the group leader and one member. The girls took turns at playing, and the nonplayers would excitedly watch the progress of the game. (As it happened, the group leader often lost points but was never completely annihilated, something the group marveled at.) The group leader was never completely opposed in this game: at least two or three girls would stand by to cheer her on and encourage her tenacity in the face of defeat (the encouragement of the mother who stands alone in the face of overwhelming odds); the five Jewish children in the group translated the Hebrew characters of the dreidel for her, consulting with one another when confused over the meaning of the letters and concerned that she not be cheated. Here the therapist was brought into the family of the group (i.e., introduced to Judaism) and instructed in the mystical language of the three Jewish members of the group.

From the first session on, the girls speculated on the nature of their therapist. Some of the girls felt that the group leader looked like a witch, like Catra, the jealous member of the fantasized leader's group. "Am I a good witch?" the leader asked. Yes, the group felt that she was, that she would be "good to little children." Someone remarked that the group leader had fuzzy hair. The two children of mixed racial identity quickly asked, assertively, "What's wrong with that?" Someone questioned, "Are you old enough to be a mother?" The opinion of the group was a unanimous "Yes." A discussion broke out as to whether the group leader should look like an adolescent or "a mommy." Hence, the group was beginning to put together a composite of qualities that their therapist (group leader) ought to have: the conflicting views were of a "cat-woman," lusty and greedy for everything, and a "mommy" who is unselfish (self-sacrificing) and good to little children.

The character Catra had the fairy-tale qualities of the stepmother: wicked (i.e., sexual) and cruel to little children, especially to the supplanted fairy-tale daughter. Thus, the stage was set for the appearance of the therapist/stepmother, the supplanter of the real (good) mother and the possessor of the spell-cast father.

The latency phase is a disguise for sexuality. To the latency age girl, as to the main character in *Alice in Wonderland,* "things are not always what they seem." People are not always what they appear to be, but some disappointments mask enchantments too.

In *The Imaginary Companion,* Nagera discusses the qualities and functions of the "imaginary companion," which to some degree parallel this group's fantasies and their projections onto the therapist. As a superego auxiliary, these fantasies (to be the sexualized cat-woman or her opposite, a good mother) may further the development of ego and superego structures. Nagera cites Selma Fraiberg, who talked about the use of the imaginary companion as scapegoat, personifying the child's vices (i.e., as Catra was used by the group of girls in this case example); as an attempt to prolong omnipotence and control; and as a primitive ego ideal. Occasionally the imaginary companion is used as a weapon for defense and provocation, motivated by loneliness and neglect. Here, in the Social Club, identification with the mythological family of women served that purpose.

The Social Club's members saw the group forming as an ideal family and made periodic references to the ideal, imaginary family of the fantasized leader and her friends. Even Catra, wicked as she was, was not a true villainess but more of a willful, wayward, self-indulgent, and therefore much-envied figure. She could act out the group's fantasies and wishes by being selfish. She also served as a means of dealing with the instinctual anxiety projected not onto a father but a mother, and she may have served as the mother who wished to act on impulse and abandon the family.

In the transference, the group began to sketch a group-idealized self-object transference. This group can be seen as hungry for idealization of a parent. (Masud Kahn has suggested that the two ingredients for the forming of the ego ideal are magical thinking and idealization by way of the ego functions.) The group now actively began to discuss the wish to form a family of their own. They began expressing disappointment with their own families and wished to create a home where the group leader would be mother and they would be sisters to one another.

Melissa was very invested in the group's beginnings. She had been a member of a previous group and was disappointed and impatient that the new group had taken so long to begin. In one session the girls had gathered around the table to work and talk, and there was a real atmosphere of intimacy and connectedness in their interaction. Melissa reached out her arms expressively and said to the group leader, "You see, I told you that this group would be a success and it is. Look at how well everyone plays together and gets along."

The group excitedly contributed endless fantasies as to how they might become a real family. Melissa, a great romantic, suggested, "Theresa [the group leader] should search and search in the streets to find us the perfect home." Someone else suggested that the group leader "buy us a brownstone and renovate it" to each group member's specification. Vicky, the oldest member and group cynic, scoffed, "How can Theresa possibly buy you all a brownstone and renovate it? Does she look like a millionaire to you? If she were a millionaire, she wouldn't be working here." At this point in its history, the group liked to repeat the leader's name (perhaps the children felt closer to her in being able to address her by her first name; the practice may also have been a means of fantasized control over the therapist).

The group enacted building a house using large blocks and a tent. The group leader remained outside of the house, waiting. This activity soon transformed itself into a different one: the girls played at rolling themselves up in foam mats. While one girl was encased in the mat, another would push at the mat, forcing out the girl within. The group leader commented that they were like caterpillars in a cocoon, coming out as butterflies. The girls seemed to have moved from the creation of a family to giving birth to themselves. Finally, the group moved into a discussion of their own families and their disillusionment with them.

In one session, one child, Rachel, described disappointment with her mother and grandfather. She had returned from a visit to her grandfather, whom she described as mean and abusive. She talked of her mother's ineffectuality in dealing with him and admitted that her life with her mother was "not so very happy." She believed that they were "going through a phase." The group leader said that adults liked to think that childhood is a happy time but that in fact it is often difficult and that when children become adults, they have somewhat more freedom of decision and choice. The group was vehemently in agreement with these observations, and one member commented that "there should be a trading post for relatives where you could trade them in for cash or a new one." This sentiment points to the intense wish of children in therapy groups to create a fantasy family so that forging a new identity for each member seems possible.

The children occasionally alluded to visits with their fathers, who were described idyllically. Becky described her father as "very handsome"; she then reported, somewhat apologetically, that he had "many girlfriends." She said that she tried to get to know them and that some were very nice; one, however, never liked her at all, but her mother told her she did not have to visit that one. Becky was wistful as she listed the many women her father had been involved with. As opposed to her father, her mother had relatively few lovers.

Rachel described her father as living "in the country" with his new family. She visited him in the summer. Rachel, like the other group members, was much taken with the wildlife of the country, especially the rabbits and deer. Like the fantasized leader's group, the girls in the Social Club described their wish to roam free in the woodlands.

All of the girls spoke of their fathers in faraway voices, as if the emotional (and, occasionally, geographic) distance made them elusive, romantic figures. Vicky had recently resurrected her relationship with her father, visiting him for the first time in many years. She was hesitant in describing her father and preferred to talk of her love for her grandmother. Vicky periodically reminded everybody that she preferred her grandmother to the leader of the group; she was fond of saying, "It's nothing against you, Theresa, but I'd rather be with my grandmother." Her maternal grandmother represented her link to an unconflicted past.

Natalie, whose mother recently remarried, refused to discuss her stepfather (or to recognize him as such at all). She frequently said she had no father. Of all the group members, Natalie eventually drew closest to the therapist and remained most intensely connected to her.

Annie Reich (1973) speaks of the great longing of the child to become like the parent as creating an inner demand on the ego. Under certain conditions, "magic identification with the glorified parent—megalomanic feelings—may replace the wish to be like [that parent]."

Vicky, in her connectedness to her grandmother, initiated discussions in the group of the Holocaust. This topic united three members in their identity. Two of the group, Rachel and Becky, were of Sephardic paternity. Rachel, identifying strongly with her Egyptian father, would break into the Egyptian dances of a harem girl whenever the group became lively over discussions involving their future sexuality. No one described losing family in the Holocaust; instead, they emphasized the reunion of their families here in America.

The theme of unification became apparent to the group leader in terms of another aspect of group members' identity. As mentioned above, the mothers of all the girls worked out of necessity and were everything to them. They worked and arranged lessons and free-time activities for their daughters. Money was a constant issue. It occurred to the therapist that the girls struggled with a central conflict: their need to unite traditional views of femininity (beauty, sexuality, and mothering) with their need to protect themselves (typically the role of the father). Freud described the two types of anaclitic (independent) object love: the "woman who tends" and "the man who protects." These girls had never known the protective aspect of family life, because their fathers were not consistently a part of their lives. As Becky said, "You don't really miss what you never knew."

The girls required of their mothers that they be all things at all times, that the exhausted mothers be transformed into superwomen. The self-object transference in therapy had the same requirement: the therapist had to be superwoman, since a disappointing therapist was intolerable. For example, during a holiday period the group did not meet for two weeks. At the next group meeting, the group was particularly angry with the therapist because of the two-week separation. Their anger was unmistakable, with everyone drawing pictures of the group leader looking like a witch, like Catra, like a monster. For one child, the conflict proved too great. She attempted to draw the group leader in a negative way as an ugly witch, but then she gave her the blue-green hair of "the watcher," the Peeka-Blue doll she had brought to the very first group meeting. She finally colored the hair over in black (the therapist's own hair color) and clothed her in the red dress of Supergirl, with a large *S* on the front of her dress. The figure is walking toward the viewer, smiling, with outstretched arms.

As the group identity solidified, the girls' latency-age-appropriate dislike of boys came to the fore. The girls heatedly debated whether or not the club should admit boys. Melissa (as usual) made an impassioned speech, saying, "We wouldn't want boys. They would only disturb the peace of our group. They would fight. They would cause mayhem." Vicky described a boy at school who was "as ugly as a belch" and who pursued girls. Natalie discovered a boy under the table in one group session (incidentally, this boy was from the boys' latency group that was held at the same time; its members periodically invaded the girls' group). She clung to the group leader's skirts but pushed her forward to make the boy leave. The boy insisted that he would be back. The group leader told him that he could not come back to this group, that he belonged to the boys' club right now. Natalie shrieked, "You hear that? You hear what she said? This is a girls' club, no boys allowed, you hear her?" She turned to the group leader, "Right? There are no boys allowed here?" The girls had all gathered around the group leader by then (not unlike avenging warriors amassing for battle). The group leader felt as if the girls had turned her into a guided missile—the role model group protector, that is, the mother who protects (as opposed to the father).

In *The Use of an Object and Relating Through Identification,* Winnicott describes the object as needing to undergo several metamorphoses. The object must be related to and destroyed by the subject, and it must finally survive the destruction. It can then be further valued as having survived destruction; having survived the subject's omnipotent control, it now can be used in fantasy. Edith Jacobson (1986, 109–19) viewed this in yet another way: identification with the aggressor is made out of fear but also out of love. The conditions for depression arise when loss of the ideal object is denied.

The group leader interpreted the Social Club's disappointment in her and anger at her as their reaction to her failure to meet with them for two weeks. The group agreed energetically that this was indeed the source of their anger. Group members subsequently had great difficulty leaving the session, and Rachel commented that she would like to "throw all the adults out of the building—even the nice ones—and leave it for the children for once."

Judith Marks Mishne has pointed out that idealization of the self and of the object is a particular feature in children who have been abandoned by a parent as a result of divorce or psychogenic illness. This is a view of idealization as a defense against mourning, where an inability to mourn is seen as a result of severe narcissistic injury. "Abandoned children manifest inordinate idealization and mirroring of the therapist, phenomena not found in children who have lost a parent through death."

Idealization of the group therapist is a defensive posture by way of identification with the aggressor (i.e., the lost father), that is, a defense against abandonment and the disappointment of being female. The Social Club members experienced intense narcissistic rage in response to the therapist's "abandonment" of the group by going on vacation; the therapist's absence was experienced by each girl as a replication of an earlier abandonment by an idealized and lost father. The therapist's abandonment was responded to by the group as an attack on the group's collective omnipotent fantasies of control over the object, in this case, the therapist.

Analysis: Theories of Play and the Group Quest for Identity

Freud described the two functions of play as trial behavior and as expression of the wish that all will turn out well. Play eases the strain of uncertainty in children about their abilities, especially as regards the future requirements of adult life. Play reflects "fragments and bits of reality." Greenacre has suggested that in play a kind of make-believe reality testing emerges.

For the girls of the Social Club, the task was to merge what they saw as the most desirable aspects of being female with the qualities they believed one needs to possess in order to survive in the real world, qualities that help to utilize aggression to defend and to protect and, when need be, to fight. A superadaptability and flexibility to survive are required. Waelder, in his theory of play, saw play as combining "mastery, wish fulfillment, assimilation of overpowering experiences (repetition/compulsion), transformation from activity to passivity, leave of absence from reality and superego, and fantasies about real objects." Franz Alexander viewed play as a creative source allowing for unlimited freedom of choice leading to experimentation.

Greenacre brilliantly summed up her two views of play: one is that play is in the service of a developing neurosis (by way of repetition compulsion); the other that it is akin to creative activity in its spontaneity and resourcefulness. In *Woman as Artist,* Greenacre talked of the high degree of bisexuality required of the artist and of "the empathic capacity of the artist to move between primary and secondary thought processes." She suggested that the gifted female child is susceptible to fantasies of the phallus (i.e., the family jewels). This is certainly one view of the Social Club's periodic identification of themselves as warrior women. Given the lack of fathering in this group, the girls' need for such a fantasy might even have been intensified.

Chasseguet-Smirgel, in discussing Anzieu's work on groups, describes the group as self-generated:

It is itself an omnipotent mother. It is not organized around a central person (the leader) but around the group itself. The group illusion is then realization of the wish to heal one's narcissistic injuries and to identify oneself with the good breast (or with the omnipotent mother) . . . the father figure is chased away . . . it is as if the group information represented the hallucinatory realization of the wish to take possession of the mother by the subship, through a very regressive mode, that of primary fusion.

A more important view must respond to the reality experienced by the mothers of members of the Social Club. The old values of women did not help them to survive or to support a child at the same time. There had been too much disappointment and failure with regard to men. It is no wonder that the girls turned (as boys do) to identification with a more powerful same-sex object. And they did so not just as identification with the aggressor but because their mothers represented their whole security from the adult world. When the family becomes a matriarchy, one's sisters become true allies. Even though the need for protection (and love) from others in the future is still intense, it is the new task of identity for girls to absorb within oneself the quality of satisfying the wish for protection.

A Latency Age Boys Group

Groups vary in personality as much as individuals do. Groups of girls tend to utilize dialogue more (while intermittently playing with games) than groups of boys. On the surface, a boy's group appears to be more action oriented, with less self-reflection. This doesn't mean, however, that the boys are less emotionally related to each other. Rather, the leader must participate in the group's activity and understand the psychodynamic meaning of the group interaction.

In a group of boys, age seven through ten, at least one child struggled with considerable anxiety and phobias. The others evinced various degrees of impulsivity. One boy, Fred, was more aggressive than the rest. He often destroyed other boys' drawings and productions, stole their snacks, and seemed to upset every group game the members participated in. When these disruptions occurred, the group leader had to enter into the group interaction and set limits for Fred. As a rule, if group members can intervene on their own and deal with a disruption in an appropriate way, it is best to allow the group process to evolve. This is also true of group discussions; if the group appears to be sustaining a long dialogue, the therapist need only interject an occasional comment to reflect or synthesize the group's feelings about a subject.

In this group, the weekly disruptions provided by Fred were leaving the other boys frustrated and angry. However, over time, a strong, articulate group member appeared to be emerging. Despite his anxieties, Mickey became the boy around whom the others coalesced. He emerged as a rival figure to Fred, whose aggression gave a degree of authority to the group as well.

During one session, the group had just begun to enthusiastically play a game when an amazing moment occurred: Mickey informed Fred quite forcefully that the boys had discussed the new game and the problems Fred had posed to the past group enterprises and that the group would now only let him participate if he agreed to follow the rules and not destroy anybody's property or smash their snacks. If Fred could agree to this, then he could play; if not, the group would not play with him any longer. The therapist acknowledged the group's right to make this decision but offered to help Fred if he found this situation too hard. Fred then agreed to the group's limit setting and asked if he could continue to participate with other members. They readily agreed.

Analysis

It was a great therapeutic triumph for Mickey and the other boys to limit Fred. Mickey had emerged as a group leader who was trusted by the other boys and encouraged to speak for them. He had learned to channel his anxieties into aggression that was protective of himself and others. He earned the respect of others not because of his physical strength but because of his ability to put into words what the other boys felt and thought. Words had become his new means of self-defense, and this new strength enabled him to speak for the group.

The therapist had to allow the group to articulate their anger at Fred. He also had to offer Fred support in controlling his impulsivity in group interactions: when Fred could no longer contain himself, the therapist would play a separate game with him.

It is important to remember that if therapy is to be helpful, it cannot be overly bound by rules and limits. Ejecting Fred from the group permanently would have been a premature act on the therapist's part. Occasionally, discussions like the one the group leader had with Fred have to be made, but therapists generally need only assist the children in a group (and occasionally direct them). By playing alone with Fred, the therapist was helping him by allowing him to have more private time, which had the effect of calming and even nurturing Fred until he could integrate himself enough to rejoin the others.

Group therapists of latency age children have to work hard at being as fair as possible. The children are, as a rule, very watchful of how supplies are divided up and how extra food is doled out. If snacks are provided, it is best to give everyone fruit or the same brand of crackers or cookies so that there are no arguments over quantity and size. Nonetheless, such arguments will occur, because children in therapy are quite regressed under the best of conditions. With deprived children, issues of food or toys become especially important.

A Group of Inner-City Children

A latency age girls' group primarily of poor inner-city children began a lively discussion of what to do if some members didn't arrive for the group session. Could they divide the absent members' snacks? The therapist described to the children the resulting problem: if she gave away the extra snacks and the members came in later, she would have no snack for them and this would be unfair. "How should we resolve this problem?" she asked the group.

By inviting a group discussion, the therapist enabled the girls to use a skill that latency age children acquire by approximately age seven: the ability to problem-solve on an abstract basis. (This group ranged in age from eight to eleven.) Children can be assisted in problem solving by encouraging them to make a list of the pros and cons of an act, think of the consequences of their actions, and associate feelings to behaviors, when it is appropriate to do so.

By age seven, children can also begin to understand what another person might feel in a certain situation. They can begin to develop empathy for others and identify with the plight of another person. This is in part a result of increased cognitive ability, but it is also an indication of the development of a superego, a conscience that dictates right from wrong. Initially, the superego might look excessively rigid in a seven-year-old. If asked about possible punishment for another child's misbehavior, a seven-year-old might suggest dire consequences that are impossibly severe. Later, however, the superego usually becomes somewhat benign.

The girls began to discuss how they might feel if they were late to the group session and found no food left. Some shared similar experiences that had happened to them. Others said that it seemed a shame to waste food if no one came. Some members wanted the therapist to take the food for herself (caring for her, as if she were in need). The therapist thanked them for thinking of her but said it was *her* job as an adult to care for *them*. The group finally decided that all extra food should be kept until it was time to go home; at that point, the extra food could be divided and shared. Although this solution was less than ideal in some respects, the discussion leading to it had allowed the group to experiment with decision making and to struggle with the idea of a sometimes unfair world.

It is an important developmental move forward for children to attempt thinking empathically about each other. This rather simple idea actually assists children in learning to control their impulses and aggression toward others. This result is probably most readily observed in group interaction. The opportunity to work out difficulties in interpersonal object relations is abundantly available in group therapy settings.

CHAPTER 20

GROUP TREATMENT
WITH ADOLESCENTS

Adolescents are more verbal than children, but they also struggle more with impulsivity. The therapist must be continually aware of the potential for acting out in adolescents in group therapy.

GROUP EXAMPLE:
MANAGING ACTING OUT IN GROUPS

In one session a group of adolescent girls were describing how much fun the group had become. Their therapist noted a degree of excitement in the girls not previously exhibited. Although alert to the dialogue, she remained silent. In a session prior to this one, the girls had complained that group was boring; the therapist had then suggested that they think about how to make it better. Some girls thought that they should meet in the park and pick up boys. Others became visibly frightened by this idea. The therapist encouraged group members to continue sharing their ideas but pointed out the difficulties that meeting in the park might pose: the girls might meet boys and would then want to end the group session, members would want to walk around and group discussion would be difficult to maintain, and so on.

In the current session, everyone seemed excited. One by one, the girls began to share something that was happening after group meetings: they had been walking together to the subway and had been "jumping the turnstiles," that is, sneaking in without paying. The therapist became alarmed but was able to control her response. She asked the group if they had thought about what might happen if they were caught. The girls discussed what an arrest might be like. The therapist noted that an arrest would jeopardize the continuation of the group, an unfortunate consequence now that the girls appeared to like their group sessions. As leader, she could not permit the continuation of a group that would be hurtful to its members. Some girls said that they wouldn't hold her responsible for this. The therapist replied that they might not but that surely their parents wouldn't permit them to attend group sessions anymore if the group helped them to get into big trouble. The girls acknowledged this. The therapist pointed out that therapy of any kind, even group, had to be helpful to its participants or it wouldn't be therapy.

Analysis

In group treatment with adolescents, group leaders must tread a tightrope. They have to be amenable to hearing about impulses of all kinds from group members, but they must neither participate in nor encourage the acting out of those impulses. For example, by laughing at inappropriate behavior or by attempting to act like an adolescent for acceptance, the leader can unwittingly contribute to and encourage acting out. This means that group leaders must ensure that they are not giving out unconscious messages to the group to act out. They also have to be comfortable with the idea that at times the group may make them an object of derision or see them as parental in negative ways. Group leaders, like therapists in individual and family work, have to become comfortable with the condition of not being loved by their clients. Of course, this is hard initially. Most child therapists love children and want to be at least liked by them. Being liked by clients is certainly desirable, and I believe that treatment and the closeness it engenders can't really be facilitated without some degree of liking. It is just that for treatment to really work, love or liking cannot always prevail as the first objective.

It is useful here to think of Winnicott's idea of the holding environment, whereby the therapist enables the client's deepest level of anxiety to be spoken and tolerated and expanded upon. Within the holding environment, the therapist facilitates a sense of safety for the client. The client can describe or talk about anything he or she chooses. The therapist can help by listening, explaining or educating where necessary, always focusing solely on the client's need.

Part V

TERMINATION

CHAPTER 21

THE TERMINATION PROCESS

Anna Freud (1980) once commented that in child treatment a complete break from the therapist makes no sense. Where children are concerned, termination involves loss of a real object as well as loss of a transference object. She recommended a gradual termination and thought that the therapist could continue to be a resource for the child.

I believe that this position makes the most sense. Children, one hopes, learn about object relations and their importance in therapy. At times a therapist might represent one of the few reliable sources of good judgment in a child's life. To cut off communications suddenly is to reinforce the kind of abandoning loss that many children have experienced all too often.

PREPARATION FOR TERMINATION

Ideally, I introduce the idea of termination when the child's symptoms have abated and the child has consolidated the gains from treatment. Prior to considering termination, the therapist can verify that the young client is functioning appropriately both in school with peers and at home. After discussion of termination with parental figures, the therapist can raise the issue with the child. In the termination process I like to review all of the things the child worked on and talked about during treatment.

Case Example

In the case of Mickey, discussed earlier in this volume, termination took roughly one year. This is not surprising, given the boy's intense anxiety about separation.

At a certain point in the treatment process, Mickey's therapist reached the conclusion that the child was functioning as well as possible. Mickey was much less constricted socially and had a number of friends. He could eat more (although this always remained an issue), and he enjoyed many after-school activities. After consultation with supervisors, the therapist reasoned that although Mickey might always have some residual difficulties, he should be free of treatment for at least some period of his life.

Mickey himself agreed that he was doing much better, but he wanted roughly one year to complete treatment and get used to functioning without his therapist.

During the termination phase, the therapist and Mickey reviewed all of his play activities in treatment sessions. His therapist connected these to issues in Mickey's life that he was struggling with at the time. Mickey periodically commented, in acknowledgment, "So that's what was happening." At one point the therapist heard an extraordinary admission from Mickey, one that assured her that he had indeed improved considerably. They were reviewing the terrifying incident that Mickey described in his first session: when big boys had chased the little boys out of the bathroom at school. Mickey then told his worker, "That's not what happened." What had actually transpired, he now revealed, was that he had *heard* about this happening to *other* boys. He then said he knew that the story couldn't be true, that there were some tough kids in his grade school and that those kids would have prevented this incident from happening and would have "taken care" of the big boys who bullied the little boys.

The therapist realized that Mickey had indeed undergone a substantial change. His reality testing had improved, so that ego boundaries were now substantiated (i.e., he now recognized that a story he had heard was different from thinking that he had actually experienced the incident in the story). Mickey now had substantially better defenses, was no longer grandiose, and was realistic about himself and his limitations. He could now trust in a sense of basic justice (basic trust).

In one session near the end of the termination phase, Mickey brought up the topic that he would soon be entering adolescence (he was eleven by this time). He had discussed this with other boys, and they had "generally agreed" that this would be the last year they would dress up in costumes for Halloween (once a feared holiday for Mickey). The therapist felt privately sad at the thought that Mickey had indeed grown up, but she supported his decision as a good one.

TERMINATION AND THE TRANSITIONAL OBJECT

At the end of treatment with child clients, some therapists choose as a parting gift a significant toy or object from the therapy room that the child was particularly attached to during treatment. If this isn't possible, the therapist can negotiate with the child about what the child might want.

Mickey requested a baseball mitt, a catcher's mitt. I felt that this was appropriate not only as evidence of his mastery of physical and psychological difficulties but also as representative of his ideals for the future (he now wanted to be a sportscaster). I remembered that in his first session he had described the best moment of his life as the one in which he had made a spectacular catch during a softball game.

It is important that the therapist not attempt to rival the child's parents or caretakers with extravagant gifts that they could not give. Rather, the therapist's gift can be seen as a form of transitional object; it is a part of the therapist that will go with the child into the future.

One child made a transitional object for her therapist on the last day of treatment. Millie was relieved of her symptoms in treatment but described her fear of termination: she said that she felt connected to her worker like a rope connected to a lifesaver. If the therapist let go, what might happen? Would she drown? The therapist told Millie that if she needed more help, she, the therapist, would always welcome Millie back. She added that Millie might think of this: what if she had learned to become a champion swimmer and didn't know it yet? Then the therapist would be holding her back by not letting her try to swim. Millie had a reaction to the idea of her autonomy; she looked very impressed and agreed that this was certainly true.

In her last session Millie constructed a key chain for her therapist. She said that she had noticed that her therapist often fumbled for her keys to the office in her bag. Millie thought that with a key chain, her therapist might find her keys faster and "could help a kid who was in trouble more quickly."

The therapist acknowledged to Millie the beauty and importance of this gift. It remained not only as a transitional object to the therapist but also as a symbol of her work and the lifeline that it represented for her.

BIBLIOGRAPHY

Aiello, T. "The Influence of the Psychoanalytic Community of Emigres (1930–1950) on Clinical Social Work with Children" in *Child and Adolescent Social Work Journal,* vol. 15, no. 2 (April 1998): 151–66.

Ainsworth, M.D.S. "Attachment: Retrospect and Prospect." In *The Place of Attachment in Human Behavior.* edited by Parkes, C. and J. Stevenson-Hinde. New York: Basic Books, 1982.

Altman, Neil. "Race, Culture and Social Class." In *The Analyst in the Inner City: Race, Class, and Culture through a Psychoanalytic Lens.* Hillsdale, NJ: The Analytic Press, 1995.

———. "Relational Perspectives on Child Psychoanalytic Psychotherapy." In *Relational Perspectives in Psychoanalysis,* edited by N. Skolnick and S. Warshaw. Hillsdale, NJ: The Analytic Press, 1992.

American Psychiatric Association. *Diagnostic and Statistical Manual of Mental Disorders* (4th ed.). Washington, DC: 1994.

Aron, Lewis. "The Relational Orientation." In *A Meeting of the Minds: Mutuality in Psychoanalysis.* Hillsdale, NJ: The Analytic Press, 1996.

———. "Relational Theory and its Boundaries." In *A Meeting of the Minds: Mutuality in Psychoanalysis.* Hillsdale, NJ: The Analytic Press, 1996.

Beebe, B. and Lachmann, F. "The Contribution of Mother-Infant Mutual Influence to the Origins of Self and Object Representations." In *Psychoanalytic Psychology,* vol. 5: 305–37.

Bollas, Christopher. *The Shadow of the Object.* London: Free Association Books, 1987.

Bowlby, J. *A Secure Base.* New York: Basic Books, 1998.

Boyd-Franklin, W. *Black Families in Therapy: A Multisystems Approach.* New York: Guilford Press, 1989.

Browne, A. "Family Violence and Homelessness: The Relevance of Trauma Histories in the Lives of Homeless Women." *American Journal of Orthopsychiatry* 63(3) (July 1993): 370–384.

Celani, D. *The Illusion of Love: Why the Battered Woman Returns to Her Abuser.* New York: Columbia University Press, 1994.

Chodorow, N. *The Reproduction of Mothering.* Berkeley: University of California Press, 1978.

Claman, L. "The Squiggle Drawing Game" in *Play Therapy Techniques* edited by C. Shaefer and D. Cangelosi. Northvale, N.J.: Jason Aronson, 1997.

Davies, J. and Frawley, M. *Treating the Adult Survivor of Childhood Sexual Abuse.* New York: Basic Books, 1994.

Esman, A. *Adolescence and Culture.* New York: Columbia University Press, 1990.

Erikson, E. "The Problem of Ego Identity." *Journal of the American Psycho-analytic Association* 4 (1956): 56–121.

Fairbairn, W.R.D. *Psychoanalytic Studies of the Personality.* London: Routledge & Kegan Paul, 1952. The repression and the return of bad objects (1943) 1941. A revised psychopathology of the psychoses and psychoneuroses.

Falco, K. *Psychotherapy with Lesbian Clients.* New York: Brunner Mazel, 1991.

Finkelhor, D. *Child Sexual Abuse: New Theory and Research.* New York: The Free Press, 1984.

ηagan, L. "Object Relations Theory." In *Inside Out and Outside In: Psy-hodynamic Clinical Theory and Practice in Contemporary Multicul-l Contexts.* Northvale, NJ: Jason Aronson, 1996.

Theory of Self Psychology." In *Inside Out and Outside In: Psy- Clinical Theory and Practice in Contemporary Multicul-* Northvale, NJ: Jason Aronson, 1996.

ted Child. Springfield, Illinois: Charles C. Thomas,

Freud, A. "The Role of Bodily Illness in the Mental Life of Children." In *Psychoanalytic Study of the Child,* vol. 7, edited by R. Eissler, A. Freud, H. Hartmann, and M. Kris. New York: International Universities Press, 1945.

Gabriel, Martha. *AIDS Trauma and Support Group Therapy.* 135–74. New York: The Free Press, 1996.

George, C. and Main, M. *"Social Interactions of Young Abused Children: Approach Avoidance and Aggression."* In *Child Development* vol. 50: 306–18.

Goldstein, E. *Ego Psychology and Social Work Practice.* 2d ed. New York: The Free Press, 1995.

Green, Arthur. *"A Psychodynamic Approach to the Study and Treatment of Child-Abusing Parents."* In Journal of the American Academy of Child Psychiatry, vol. 15 (1976): 414–29.

———. "The Abused Child and Adolescent." In *Handbook of Clinical Assessment of Children and Adolescents,* vol. 11. Edited by C. Kestenbaum and T. Williams. New York: New York University Press, 1988.

Greenson, R. "On Transitional Objects and Transference." In *Between Reality and Fantasy. Transitional Objects and Phenomena,* edited by Grolnick, S. and L. Borkin. New York: Jason Aronson, 1978.

Grossman, Arnold. "Homophobia: A Cofactor of HIV Disease in Gay and Lesbian Youth." *Journal of the Association of Nurses in AIDS Care* vol. 5, no. 1 January–February 1994.

Herman, J. *Trauma and Recovery.* New York: Basic Books, 1992.

Herman, J., Perry, C., VanderKolk, B. "Childhood Trauma in Borderline Personality Disorders." In *American Journal of Psychiatry* (April 1989): 490–95.

Hunt, Robert. "Attention Deficit Disorder and Hyperactivity." In *Handbook of Clinical Assessment of Children and Adolescents,* vol. 7: Edited by C. Kestenbaum and T. Williams. New York: New York University Press, 1988.

Hunter, S., Shannon, C., Knox, J., Martin, J.I. *Lesbian, Gay and Bi-sexual Youth and Adults: Knowledge for Human Service Practice.* Thousand Oaks, CA: Sage, 1998.

Irvine, J., ed. *Sexual Cultures and the Construction of Adolescent Identities.* Philadelphia: Temple University Press, 1991.

Jacobson, E. *The Self and the Object World.* Madison, CT: International Universities Press, 1986.

Kernberg, P. "Children in Borderline Personality Organization." In *Handbook of Clinical Assessment of Children and Adolescents,* vol. 7, edited by C. Kestenbaum and T. Williams. New York: New York University Press, 1988, 604–25.

Kestenbaum, C., and T. Williams, eds. *Handbook of Clinical Assessment of Children and Adolescents.* Vol. II. New York: New York University Press, 1988.

Klein, M. "The Importance of Symbol Formation in the Development of the Ego." In *Love, Guilt and Reparation and Other Works 1921–45.* 219–32. New York: Delta, 1975.

Kohut, H. *The Analysis of the Self.* New York: International University Press, 1971.

———. *The Kohut Seminars on Self Psychology and Psychotherapy with Adolescents and Young Adults,* edited by M. Elson, 260–80. New York: W. W. Norton, 1987.

Lichtenberg, J., Lachman F., and Fosshage, J. *Self and Motivational Systems: Toward a Theory of Psychoanalytic Technique.* Hillsdale, NJ: Analytic Press, 1992.

Loewald, H. W. Quoted in M. Kahn, "Ego Ideal, Excitement, and the Threat of Annihilation." In *The Privacy of the Self,* edited by M. Kahn, pp. 193–94. New York: International Universities Press, 1974.

Mahler, M. *The Memoirs of Margaret Mahler.* New York: The Free Press, 1988.

Mahler, M., Pine, F., and A. Bergman. *The Psychological Birth of the Human Infant.* New York: Basic Books, 1975.

McNamee, S. "Reconstructing Identity: The Communal Construction of Crisis." In *Therapy as Social Construction,* edited by S. McNamee and K. Geigen, 186–99. London: Sage Publications, 1992.

Meeks, J. "Substance Abuse Disorders." In *Child Psychopathology: A Social Work Perspective,* edited by F. Turner. New York: The Free Press, 1989.

Menaker, E. *Appointment in Vienna.* New York: St. Martin's Press, 1989.

Minuchin, S. *Families of the Slums.* New York: Basic Books, 1967.

————. *Families and Family Therapy.* Cambridge, Mass.: Harvard University Press, 1974.

Mishne, Judith Marks. *The Learning Curve: Elevating Children's Academic and Social Competence.* Northvale, NJ: Jason Aronson, 1996.

————. *Clinical Work with Children.* New York: The Free Press, 1983.

————. *Clinical Work with Adolescents.* New York: The Free Press, 1986.

Mitchell, S. "The Relational Matrix." In *Relational Concepts in Psychoanalysis: An Integration.* Cambridge, Mass.: Harvard University Press, 1988.

————. Part III: Infantilism. In *Relational Concepts in Psychoanalysis.* Cambridge, Mass.: Harvard University Press, 1988.

Moskowitz, M. "The Social Conscience of Psychoanalysis." In *Reaching Across Boundaries of Culture and Class: Widening the Scope of Psychotherapy,* edited by R. Perez-Foster, M. Moskowitz, and R. A. Javier. Northvale, NJ: Jason Aronson, 1996.

Nielsen, Kay (illustrator). *East of the Sun and West of the Moon.* New York: Doubleday, 1977.

Osden, T. *Projective Identification and Psychotherapeutic Technique.* New York: Jason Aronson, 1982.

Perez-Foster, R. "Assessing the Psychodynamic Functions of Language in the Bilingual Student." In *Reaching Across Boundaries of Culture and Class: Widening the Scope of Psychotherapy,* edited by R. Perez-Foster, M. Moskowitz, and R. A. Javier. Northvale, NJ: Jason Aronson, 1996.

Phillips, A. *Winnicott.* Cambridge, Mass.: Harvard University Press, 1988.

Pine, F. "Borderline in Children: A Clinical Essay." *Psychoanalytic Study of the Child* 29 (1974): 391–468.

Reich, A. "Narcissistic Object Choice in Women." In *Psychoanalytic Contributions.* New York: International Universities Press, 1973.

Sandler, J., Kennedy, H., and R. L. Tyson. *The Technique of Child Psychoanalysis: Discussion with Anna Freud.* Cambridge, Mass.: Harvard University Press, 1980.

Sbriglio, R., Hartman, N., Millman, R., and Khuri, E. "Drug and Alcohol Abuse in Children and Adolescents." In *Handbook of Clinical Assess-*

ment of Children and Adolescents, edited by C. Kestenbaum and T. Williams. New York: New York University Press, 1988.

Schaefer, C. and O'Connor, K., eds. *Handbook of Play Therapy.* New York: John Wiley & Sons, 1983.

Seinfeld, Jeffrey. "Handling the Negative Therapeutic Reaction in the Treatment of Children." In *The Bad Object: Handling the Negative Therapeutic Reaction in Psychotherapy.* Northvale, NJ: Jason Aronson, 1995.

Seligman, S. "Historical Legacies and Contemporary Innovation." *Psychoanalytic Dialogues,* vol. 7, no. 6 (1997). Symposium in Child Analysis.

Siskind, D. *Working with Parents.* Northvale, NJ: Jason Aronson, 1997.

Skolnick, N. and Warshaw, S., eds. *Relational Perspectives in Psychoanalysis.* Hillsdale, NJ: The Analytic Press, 1992.

Spotnitz, H. "Transference and Countertransference in Group Therapy." In *Modern Psychoanalysis* vol. 12, no. 1, 25–34.

Stern, D. *The Interpersonal World of the Infant.* New York: Basic Books, 1985.

Stolorow, R. "On Experiencing an Object: A Multidimensional Perspective." In *Progress in Self Psychology,* vol. 2, edited by A. Goldberg, 273–79. New York: Guilford Press, 1986.

———. "Daring to Desire: Culture and the Bodies of Adolescent Girls." In *Sexual Cultures and the Construction of Adolescent Identities,* edited by J. Irvine. Philadelphia: Temple University Press.

Verhulst, F. C. "Diagnosing Borderline Children." In *Acta Paedopsychiatry.* Vol. 50: 161–73. Cited in Kernberg, P. "Children in Borderline Personality Organization." In *Handbook of Clinical Assessment of Children and Adolescents,* vol. 7. Edited by C. Kestenbaum and T. Williams, 604–25. New York: New York University Press, 1988.

Warshaw, S. "Mutative Factors in Child Psychoanalysis: A Comparison of Diverse Relational Perspectives." In *Relational Perspectives in Psychoanalysis,* edited by N. Skolnick and S. Warshaw. Hillsdale, NJ: The Analytic Press, 1992.

Webb, N. B., N. Wilson, and E. Zigler. *Social Work Practice with Children.* New York: Guilford Press, 1996.

Western, Drew, Ludolph, Misle, Ruffins, Block. "Physical and Sexual Abuse in Adolescent Girls with Borderline Personality Disorder." *American*

Journal Orthopsychiatric Association, Inc., vol. 60, no. 1 (January 1990):

Winnicott, D. W. "The Squiggle Game." In *Therapeutic Consultations in Child Psychiatry.* New York: Basic Books, 1971.

———. "Hate in the Countertransference." In *Through Pediatrics to Psychoanalysis.* London: Hogarth, 1958.

———. "Ego Distortion in Terms of the True and False Self." In *The Maturational Process and the Facilitating Environment.* New York: International University Press, 1965.

———. "The Use of an Object and Relating Through Identifications." In *Playing and Reality.* Middlesex, England: Penguin, 1974.

———. "Communicating and not Communicating Leading to a Study of Certain Opposites." In *The Maturational Process and the Facilitating Environment.* New York: International University Press, 1965.

INDEX

Abandoned children, 88
  anxiety, 70–71, 110
  depression, 173, 174
  grief, 173
  and idealization of self, 189
  parents, 144, 165, 172, 173, 174
  and rescue fantasies, 114
  themes, 114
  by therapist, 189
  transference, 20
Abuse, defined, 72
  of parents, 159
  severe, 84, 86
Abused adolescents, 16
Abused children
  characteristics of, 72–73
  and negative therapeutic reaction, 65–66
  and play, 63, 64
  and relationships, 4
  thinking they are bad, 16
Abusive children, 177
Abusive parents, 72
Acting out behavior, 98
  current use of term, 35
  definitions, 35
  distinguishing, 25–28
  in group therapy, 178, 196–98
  patterns, 35
  by therapist, 114–15
  upsetting to therapist, 116
Action, 25–28
Activity group therapy, 177, 180
Adolescence
  and depression, 20, 21
  myth of, 12
  pathologies of, 16
  and self psychology, 23–25

Adolescent assessment, 36–38
Adolescent homosexuality, 137–38
Adolescent therapy
  AIDS client, 129–31
  choosing acting out, 25, 26–27
  diagnostic assessment, 51–56
  first interview, 33–39
  first session, 51–56
  history, 51–56
  multicultural issues, 152–54
  Posttraumatic Stress Disorder, 91–94
  sexual identity, 137–38
Adolescents
  acting as parents, 20, 22
  and bad, exciting object, 16–20
  choice of actions, 27–28
  diagnostic assessment of, 33–39
  dissociative state, 91
  need for vindication, 20–21, 23
  perception of reality, 10
  severely disturbed, 73
  and sexuality, 132–36
  and suicide, 17, 24
Adoption, 140–48
Affective exhilaration, 19
Aggression, 73, 88, 89
  in group therapy, 192, 193
  negative therapeutic reaction, 64,
    65–66
  and residential treatment, 169, 172,
    177
Aichhorn, August, 13, 14
AIDS, 132
AIDS patient, 129–31
Ainsworth, M. D. S., 4, 5
Alcoholic parents, children of, 103–
    104

Alexander, Franz, 190
Alternative self, 92
Altman, Neil, 62–63, 132
American Psychiatric Association, 77
Amnesia, 91
Antisocial behavior, 73, 79–80
Antisocial children, 64–66
Anxiety
    disorder, 78, 85
    excessive, 42–43
    free-floating, 74
    and Posttraumatic Stress Disorder, 83
Aries, Philippe, 12
Aron, Lewis, 6, 103
Asperger's Disorder, 75
Assuming new identity, 91
Attachment theory, 15
Attention Deficit Disorder with Hyperactivity (ADHD), 86, 97–98
Attention span, 49
Autism, 75
Autonomous functioning, 28, 110, 138
    choosing action, 25
    and physical illness, 125
    respect for, 9, 130, 131

Bad, exciting object, 16–20, 21, 105
    attachment, 89
    ties, 19
Basic trust, 203
Bateson, 160
Beebe, Beatrice, 5, 6
Behavioral disturbances, 84
Bettelheim, Bruno, 113
Bilingual assessment, 155–56
Biological parents, fantasies about, 144
Bipolar model, 5
Bizarre delusions, 42
Blos, Peter, 13, 14
Bollas, Christopher, 108, 111–12
Books for play therapy, 59
Borderline child, 42–43
    family therapy, 82
    fantasies, 80–81
    outpatient treatment, 80–82
    play of, 81
    residential treatment, 79–80
    symptoms of, 78
Borderline Personality Disorder (BPD),
    78, 83, 84
Borderline states, 77–82
Bowlby, J. A., 4, 5, 15, 173

British Object Relations Theory, 4–5
Burnout of therapists, 131

Castration anxiety, 125
Celani, David, 18
Central nervous system abnormalities, 75
Chasseguet-Smirgel, 190–91
Child abuse, 72–73
Child therapy
    abused children, 64
    countertransference, 113–21
    diagnostic assessment, 29–32, 43–51
    first interview, 29–32
    first session, 40–51
    use of metaphor, 68–69
    mid phase of treatment, 63–64
    multicultural issues, 149–52
    use of play, 68–69
    Posttraumatic Stress Disorder, 88,
        94–96
    process of, 30
    transference, 106–11
Childhood disintegration disorder, 75
Childhood disorders, 74
Childhood psychoses, 75
Childhood schizophrenia, 75
Childhood trauma, 84
Children
    dreams of, 41
    fears of, 40
    with life-threatening illnesses, 127–29
    parentified, 20, 22
    perception of reality, 9–10
    self-soothing mechanisms, 24
Chodorow, N., 81
Client-therapist relationship, 7
Climate of pathology, 72–73
Clinical social work and relational therapy, 9
Code language, 170
Cognitive disruption, signs of, 85
Cognitive functioning and trauma, 84,
    85
Cognitive functioning tests, 39
Common themes for groups, 177
Compulsion to reenact trauma, 88
Compulsive repetition, 50, 84–85
Concrete play, 85
Concrete thinking, 76, 77, 175
Conduct Disorder, 78
Confidentiality following adolescent
    assessment, 36

Countertransference, 88, 108, 113–21
    and false self, 119–20
    hate, 117
    idealizing, 117
    manic defense, 114–115
Crafts for play therapy, 59
Cruelty to children, 73
Cultural differences, 9, 22–23
    and adoption, 147
    child rearing, 160
    in treatment, 149–56
Cutting of body, 34

Death of child or adolescent, 125–32
Death, witnessing, 85, 86, 87, 88
Decompensation, 172, 176
Delinquency, 14
    adolescents, 16–18
    midphase treatment, 17
    relationship to fathers, 18
Denial, 14, 15
    as defense, 73
    of foster parents, 142–43
    of ill childen, 126
    of loss, 189
Depression
    of abused children, 73, 74
    of adolescents, 20, 21, 23, 51, 52
    and Attention Deficit Disorder with
        Hyperactivity, 98
    chronic and Posttraumatic Stress Dis-
        order, 83, 84
    and gay adolescents, 137–38
    and group therapy, 179
    of parents affects child, 103–104, 161,
        172
    of therapist, 121
Destructive children, 169
Developmental history, 37–38
Developmental theories, 6
*Diagnostic and Statistical Manual of Men-
    tal Disorders* (DSM–IV), 77–78, 90
Diagnostic assessment,
    adolescents, 33–39
    children, 29–32, 34, 43–51
Disorganized behavior, 98
Dissociative fantasy state, 92, 93
Dissociative Fugue, 90, 91
Dissociative Identity Disorder, 90–94
Dissociative states, 90–94
Distractibility, 98
Divorce and the child, 161–62, 163

Dolls for play therapy, 58, 60
Drawings by children, 40, 67
    of family, 30–31, 154
    of home, 31
Dreams, children's, 41, 66, 155
Dreidel game, 182–83
Dying child or adolescent, 125–32
Dyslexic adolescent, 152–154

Early infant-caregiver relations, 4, 6
East of the Sun and West of the Moon,
    147
Eating, compulsive, 81
Eating disorder, 40–51, 69
Ego, a future for, 181, 183, 184
"The Ego and the Id," 3
Ego boundaries, 203
Ego defenses, 14
Ego functions, 13
Ego psychology, 3–4, 6
    and child therapy, 13
    and early adolescence theorists, 13
Elson, Miriam, 74
Emotional abuse, 32, 85
Emotional deprivation, 72
Emotional separation, 70, 71
Empathic mirroring, 77
Empathy in group therapy, 194, 195
Encopresis, 74
Eneuresis, 74, 141–42
Erickson, Erik, 3–4, 13, 14, 144–45
Escalona, S., 98
Esman, A., 132
Eye contact, 42, 73

Fairbairn, W. R. D., 4, 15
    bad object, 105
    concept of moral defense, 16–18
    and hysterics, 93
    psychopathologies as techniques, 74
False self, 119–20
Families in poverty, 20
Families oppressed by racism, 20
Family
    cultural values, 52–53
    at first interview, 29–30
    history, 34
    not at first interview, 33
    system, 160–61
    therapy sessions, 43, 82
    treatment, 94–96, 159–67
    violence, 52, 53, 54

Fantasies
  of borderline child, 80–81
  of ill children, 126
  of therapy group, 180–81, 185, 186
  of total control, 89
  of vindication, 21
Fears of children, 43, 45, 46
  of contagion, 85
  of death, 42, 50, 125, 129
  and use of metaphor, 69–70
Female adolescents and sexuality, 132–36
Fenichel, 25
Fetishes of children, 43, 45
Finkelhor, D., 84
First session techniques, 35–36
  with adolescent, 51–56
  with child, 40–51
Forensic interview and assessment, 54–56
Fosshage, James, 5, 8
Foster care, multiple placements, 139–40
Foster care, and multiple trauma, 120–21
Foster child's scrapbook, 139–40
Fragmentation, 76, 171
Fraiberg, Selma, 184
Franklin, Boyd, 151–52
Free-floating anxiety, 74
Freud, Anna, 51
  and adolescence, 13, 14
  and effect of physical illness, 125
  and ego, 3
  and play therapy, 57
  on termination, 201
  and transference, 10–11
Freud, Sigmund, 3
  and acting out, 25, 35
  analytical object love, 187
  and depression, 93
  functions of play, 190
Frustration, of therapist, 121

Games for play therapy, 58, 59, 69–70
Gay adolescents, 137–38
Geershenson, 139
Gender differences, 9
George, C., 73
Goal achievement, and Posttraumatic
  Stress Disorder, 84
Golden, D., 125
Grandiose self, 23, 24
Grandiosity, 5, 14
  adolescent, 17
  of child, 31

as defense, 15, 73
fantasy of total control, 89
and shame, 23, 24
therapist's, 103, 115
when ill, 126
Green, Arthur, 72, 73
Greenacre, 25, 190
Greenberg, Joanne, 127
Greenson, R., 71
Group as family, 182
Group games, 60, 62
Group identity, 188
Group therapy
  for adolescent girls, 196–98
  for boys, 191–93
  for girls, 179–91
  for ill children, 126
  for inner-city girls, 193–95
  racial differences, 150–54
Group treatment for children, 177–95
Guilt
  about parents separating, 42
  due to abuse, 94
  and acting out, 25
  of ill children, 126
  and intrapsychic vendetta, 21
  of therapist, 149
Guntrip, 4

Haley, 160
Hallucinations and borderline child,
  42
Hartmann, 3
Hatred of patients, 117
Heimann, Paula, 108
Helplessness of therapist, 121
Herman, J., 83, 84
Holding environment, 198
Homosexuality, 137–38
Hospices and multiple trauma, 120–21
Hostility, first session, 35
Housing problems, 72
Hunter, S., 138
Hyperactivity, 86, 97
  and play therapy, 98
  and sexual abuse, 94
Hyperbole, use of, 174
Hypervigilance, 73

I Never Promised You a Rose Garden
  (Greenberg), 127
Id impulses, 13–14

Idealization, 5, 15
  in countertransference, 117
  in transference, 104–105
Idealized self-object transference, 24–25
Idealizing transference, resolution,
  111
Identity formation, 179
Identity issues in adopted children,
  145–48
Identity and Posttraumatic Stress Disor-
  der, 83
Imaginary Companion, The (Nagera),
  184
Immigrant families, 20
Impulse disordered children in residen-
  tial treatment, 168–69
Impulsivity, 83, 97
Inability to concentrate, 97
Inability to learn new skills, 74
Inappropriate behavior, 75
Infant research, 4–5
Inner-city children, 38
Interpersonal
  difficulties, and group therapy,
    179
  problems, and Posttraumatic Stress
    Disorder, 83
  relationships, and sexual abuse, 93
Intrapsychic vendetta, 20–23
IQ tests, 39

Jackson, 160
Jacobson, Edith, 189
Joblessness of parents, 72

Kahn, Masud, 184
Kernberg, Paulina, 78, 81
Kingston, Maxine Hong, 180
Klein, Melanie, 4, 15
  and concrete thought, 76
  symbolic thinking, 175
Kohut, Heinz, 5, 15, 74
  choosing action, 25
  lack of mirroring, 105
  and primary disorder of self, 76
  and shame, 23–24
Kübler-Ross, Elisabeth, 129

Lachmann, Frank, 5
Learning disabilities, 84, 97–99
Lichtenberg, Joseph, 5–6
Little, Margaret, 108

Loewald, H. W., 181
Loss of real object, 201
Loss of transference object, 201
Low self-esteem, 8
Lying, 81

Magical thinking, 126, 184
Mahler, Margaret, 4–5, 6, 13
Main, M., 73
Malnutrition, 72
Manic defense, 114–15
Marital discord, 52
Masturbation, 49, 74
Metaphors, 60–61, 146
  in therapy, 174, 175
  and transitional object, 71
Metapsychological Profile, 51
Minuchin, 73
Mishne, Judith Marks, 189
Mistrust, 91
Mitchell, Stephen, xii, 6, 73
Model scene, 22
Motivational systems of psyche, 6
Multicultural issues, 51–54, 149–56
Multilingual children, 154–55
Multiple Personality Disorder, 90
Multiple placements in foster care,
  139–40
Mutuality, 103

Natural disaster, witnessing, 85
Negative therapeutic reaction, 64–66
Neglect of children, 72, 114
Neurological examination, 34
New adoptive parents, 142–43
Night (Wiesel), 84
Nightmares, 41, 86

Object constancy, 5, 14–15
Object of play, the therapist as, 67–68
Object relations theory, 4, 15, 201
Objective countertransference, 114
Obsessional thinking, 42
Open-ended questions, 31
Oral aggression, 43, 45
Other-centered listening perspective,
  8
Outpatient treatment of adolescent,
  88

Panic of ill children, 126
Panphobic child, 69

Parental inconsistency, 78
Parentified children, 20, 22, 31
Parents
    alcoholic, 79–80, 82, 103–104
    and developmental history, 36
    and displaced anger, 162
    depressed, 103–104
    in family therapy, 160
    helplessness and child's abuse, 95
    marital difficulties, 42, 43, 46
    suicide attempts, 51–52
    therapist identifying with, 115–16
Pathologies of adolescence, 16
Perez-Foster, R., 154, 155
Personal prejudices of therapist, 7
Pervasive Developmental Disorders
    (PDD), 75–77, 169–76
Phillips, Adam, 106, 108
Phobias, of children, 43, 45, 50
Physical abuse
    of children, 14, 32
    and Posttraumatic Stress Disorder, 34,
        85, 86
    and rescue fantasies, 114
Physical deprivation, 72
Physical development, of child, 48
Physical illness, effect on client, 125–32
Physical trauma, 72
Physically abusive fathers and delinquent
    boys, 18
Physician's report, 4
Pine, Fred, 79
Play
    interpretation of, 66–68
    repetitive, 62
    theories of, 61–63, 190
    value of, 57
Playing house, 62
Play therapy, 30, 57–71
    and hyperactivity, 98
    interpretation of, 63–64
    and metaphor, 60–61
    negative therapeutic reaction, 64–66
    play materials, 57–60
    and Posttraumatic Stress Disorder,
        84–90
Posttraumatic Stress Disorder (PTSD),
    83–96
    aftereffects, 83–84
    and family treatment, 94–96
    and interpersonal relationships,
        62

    and murder scene, 62
    and play therapy, 84–90
    and stressors, 85–86
Poverty, 72
Precocious sexuality, 74
Preoccupation with death/disaster, 43,
    45
Preparation for termination, 201–203
Primary process thinking, 169
Primitive devaluation, 15
Problem solving in group therapy, 194
Projection, 14, 18
    by children, 15
    as defense, 73
    by parents, 81, 166
    and social classes, 132–33
Projective identification, 15
Projective tests, 39
Psyche, 5, 6–7
Psychiatric interview, 34
Psychoanalysis, xi–xii, 11
Psychoanalytic theory, 3
Psychogenic Fugue, 90
Psycholinguistic assessment of bilingual
    clients, 155
Psychological intervention, and ill chil-
    dren, 125
Psychological testing, 34, 38–39
Psychopathology, 72–82
Psychoses in childhood, 75–82
Psychotherapy, xi, xiii–xiv, 9
Psychotic behavior encouraged by
    parents, 79
Psychotic children in residential treat-
    ment, 168–69
Punitive discipline of children, 73

Racial differences, 9, 150–54
Racism, 72
Rages, 74
Reality testing, 84
Reframing, 164, 165
Regression, 172–73
    caused by illness, 125
    and change in living conditions,
        141
    of group, 121
    in group therapy, 193
Reich, Annie, 187
Rejection, 73
Relatedness, lack of in adolescent, 55,
    56

Relational development, 96
Relational theory, 3–6, 12–28
Relational therapists, 74
Relational therapy, 3–11, 63
Relational treatment, 92–93
Relationships, 4, 84, 86
Religious differences, 9
Repeated trauma, 85
Repetition compulsion, 16, 27
Repetitive behavior, 84, 165
Repetitive play, 62, 86, 87
Reporting at-risk behavior, 90
Repression, 13–14, 154, 168
Rescue fantasies of therapist, 114–15
Residential treatment, 168–76
    and Borderline Personality Disorder,
      78
    and multiple trauma, 120–21
    and Posttraumatic Stress Disorder,
      86
Resistance, 154
Rigid behavior, 75
Ritualized play, 85
Rituals, 43, 45
Rorschach test, 39
Running away, 34, 84, 172, 173
Rural children, 38

Sandler, J., 10–11, 110
Scapegoating
    and Asperger's Disorder, 75
    by children, 168, 170, 177–78
    in family, 14, 72, 73, 161–62, 165
    of imaginary companion, 184
Schizophrenia, as adult, 75
Scouting programs, 99
Secondary process thinking, 169
Secondary trauma, 120–21, 131
Seinfeld, Jeffrey, 64, 109
Self-deprecation, 73
Self-destructive behavior, 34, 73
Self-esteem, 83
    developing, 171
    poor, 23, 24, 97
Self-identity in toddlers, 5
Self-object transference, 187
Self-objects in childhood, 5
Self-protection, 179–80
Self psychology, 5–6
    and adolescence, 23–25
    current ideas, 15
    and repetitive behavior, 74

Self-regulation, 7–8
Self-representation, 5, 96, 125–26
Sense of self, 8
Separation anxiety, 69, 110
    child's, 42, 43
    parent's, 44, 46
    and hospitalization, 125
Separation-individuation, 4
Severe deprivation, 120–21
Sexual abuse
    of adolescent, 88
    and Borderline Personality Disorder,
      84
    of children, 14, 32, 72
    and Posttraumatic Stress Disorder, 34,
      85
    and rescue fantasies, 114
Sexual orientation, 9, 137–38
Sexuality, 132–39
Shame
    adolescent, 21, 22
    pervasive, 23, 24
    profound sense of, 86
    due to sexual abuse, 94, 95
    and sexual identity problem, 137
    of therapist, 149
Shapiro, R., 73
Silence during sessions, 35
Single mothers, 162–67, 187–88
Single-parent families, 179
Siskind, D., 82
Slavson, S. R., 180
Sleep problems, 46, 48, 83
Smiling, and oral aggression, 42, 43, 45
Social changes and sexual revolution, 132
Social class differences, 9
Social classes and projection, 132–33
Social constructivism, 9–11
Social stressors, 14, 72
Splitting, 14, 73
    by therapist, 114–15, 159
Sponge balls for play therapy, 59
Spouse abuse, 72
Stanford-Binet test, 39
Stereotyped behavior, 75
Stern, Daniel, 5, 6, 15
Subjective countertransference, 116
Sublimation, 171–72
Substance abuse, 72, 79–80, 82
    and Attention Deficit Disorder with
      Hyperactivity, 98
    and gays, 138

Suicidal ideation, 17
  and diagnostic assessment, 34
  and gay adolescents, 137–38
  and Posttraumatic Stress Disorder, 83, 84
  and violence to others, 73
Superego, 194
Superheroes and superheroines, 180
Symbolic thinking, 175

Termination process, 201–204
Terr, Lenore, 84–85
Tests for learning disabilities, 38–39
Tests for organic impairments, 38–39
Thematic Apperception Test (TAT), 39
Therapists
  and guilt, rage, 121
  hating clients, 117
  idealizing countertransference, 117–19
  in loco parentis, 113, 118–19
  as object, 11
  as object of play, 67–68, 71
  as parental figures, 116
Therapist's burnout, 131
Therapist's role
  as advocate, 32, 82
  as affirmer of reality, 93, 140, 154
  and Attention Deficit Disorder with
    Hyperactivity, 98
  as educator, 64
  as empathizer, 7, 8, 26, 77
  in group therapy, 178, 191, 193, 197
  with ill patients, 126, 131
  as interpreter, 106
  listening to traumas, 88
  as new and old object, 62–63
  and personal prejudices, 7
  as provider of groundedness, 139–40
  with psychotic child, 169
  in residential treatment, 175
  in role reversal, 110
  to tolerate regression, 113
  as transformational object, 107, 108,
    111–12
  to validate perceptions, 126, 127
  to work with parents, 159–60
Therapy and use of metaphor, 68–69
Therapy and use of play, 68–69
Threats of physical harm, 85
Three wishes, of children, 31, 41
Tolman, D., 133

Tolpin, 74
Toys for play therapy, 57–60
Transference, 22, 103–12
  adolescent's fantasies, 92, 93
  of child, 71
  and child's fantasy, 141
  in classical psychoanalysis, 11
  as communication, 105–106
  development of, 106–111
  group-idealized, 184
  idealization in, 104–105
  and language choice, 154
  resolution, 111
  of therapy group, 181
  to work through the past, 77
Transformational object, 111–12
Transitional object, 109–10, 181
  gifts, 203–204
  as metaphor, 71
Trauma
  and play, 86, 87, 88
  and repetition compulsion, 25
  and rescue fantasies, 114
  survivors, 83–96
Trauma-specific fears, 84, 85, 86
Treatment goal, 36
Treatment phases
  beginning, 3–99
  last phase, 109
  middle, 21–22, 103–21
  termination, 201–204
Truancy, 152, 172

Unavailable mothers, and delinquent
  boys, 18
Undersocialized children, 64
Understanding clients, 7
Urban children, 38
*Use of an Object and Relating Through
  Identification, The* (Winnicott),
  188–89

VanderKolk, 84, 88, 95
Verhalst, F. C., 78
Vindication, 23
Violence expected in relationships, 73
Violence in family, 14, 52, 53, 54
Violent behavior, 54, 79–80, 169
Visualized memories, 84

Waelder, 190
War, witnessing, 85

Warshaw, S., 11
Wechsler Intelligence Scale for Children
  (WISC), 39
Well-timed interpretation, 66
Wiesel, Elie, 84
Winnicott, D. W., 4, 15, 66
  hate in countertransference, 117

holding environment, 198
interpreting too much, 106, 108
and transitional object, 71
true and false self, 81
Woman as Artist (Greenacre), 190
Woman Warrior, The, 152, 180
Working diagnosis/hypothesis, 34

Printed in the United States
20996LVS00007B/157-204